WHY PRAY?

WHY PRAY?

INSIGHTS on the

PURPOSE, POWER, and PRIORITY

of PRAYING!

Compiled and Written by
Tom McDonald

Alpharetta, Georgia

Although the author has made every reasonable effort to ensure that the information in this book is correct, the author does not assume and hereby disclaims any liability to any party for any loss, damage, or disruption caused by errors or omissions, whether such errors or omissions result from negligence, accident, or any other cause. The author has made every effort to give credit to the source of any quotes or other material contained within and obtain permissions when feasible.

Copyright © 2023 by Thomas B. McDonald III

All rights reserved. No part of this book may be reproduced or transmitted in any form or by any means, electronic or mechanical, including photocopying, recording, or any information storage and retrieval system, without permission in writing from the author. However, permission is granted for anyone to faithfully use portions of this book as may be required to teach from it. I do not grant permission to modify the book or its contents in any way. You must use it as it is written.

ISBN: 978-1-6653-0745-1 - Paperback
eISBN: 978-1-6653-0746-8 - eBook

These ISBNs are the property of Heavenly Light Press (a Division of BookLogix) for the express purpose of sales and distribution of this title. The content of this book is the property of the copyright holder only. Heavenly Light Press does not hold any ownership of the content of this book and is not liable in any way for the materials contained within. The views and opinions expressed in this book are the property of the Author/Copyright holder, and do not necessarily reflect those of Heavenly Light Press/BookLogix.

Library of Congress Control Number: 2023917377

Printed in the United States of America

♾This paper meets the requirements of ANSI/NISO Z39.48-1992 (Permanence of Paper)

Scriptures quoted are either from the New American Standard Bible or the New Living Translation Bible. Permissions follow:
Scripture taken from the NEW AMERICAN STANDARD BIBLE ®, Copyright © 1960, 1962, 1963, 1968, 1971, 1972, 1973, 1975, 1977, 1995 by the Lockman Foundation. Used by permission.
Scripture taken from the Holy Bible, New Living Translation, copyright © 1966, 2004. Used by permission of Tyndale House Publishers, Inc., Wheaton, Illinois 60189. All rights reserved.

Quotation of E.M. Bounds from the book "Power Through Prayer", copyright © 2009, is permitted by Moody Publishers, Chicago, Illinois 60610

Quotations of Dr. Lehman Strauss from the book "Sense and Nonsense About Prayer", copyright © 1974, is permitted by Moody Publishers, Chicago, Illinois 60610

Quotation of Keith Ferguson from the book "Rise Up and Praise Him", copyright © 2020, created and compiled by Phil Barfoot, is permitted by CCT Publishing, Franklin, TN 37067

Quotation of the Kendrick Brothers from their book "The Battle Plan for Prayer", copyright © 2015, is permitted by Lifeway Christian Resources, Brentwood, TN 37027

Quotations of Larry Lea, *Could You Not Tarry One Hour* (Lake Mary, FL: Charisma House, 1987), Used by permission.

Taken from *New Morning Mercies* by Paul David Tripp, Copyright © 2014, pp. April 2 - 538; April 30 - 270; May 7 - 69; June 12 - 149; Total 1026. Used by permission of Crossway, a publishing ministry of Good News Publishers, Wheaton, IL 60187, www.crossway.org.

The Prayer of Healing in Prayer Points by Jon Graf, used by permission from the Church Prayer Leader's Network.

ACKNOWLEDGMENTS

This book would not have been written if my church had not asked me to be part of a teacher-team going to help Evangelical Pastors of poor churches in a part of the Yucatan Peninsula of Mexico in 2011. Having spent the effort to compile and write a teaching manuscript for my use there and later in my home church, it recently occurred to me that these excellent materials needed to be shared with a wider group of people. Thus this book.

I must acknowledge the truly exceptional value of the material from so many quoted insightful thinkers, writers and pray-ers on this vast and precious subject of Praying. As Dr. Lehman Strauss says (and my experience supports), this subject, the Christian Discipline of Praying, is not in great favor within many churches today. He goes on to say with many proofs, that's probably one of the principal reasons so many of our churches are weak and failing. This book is designed to be a teaching tool for those who care to use it as such. This book is much richer for that important purpose because of their insights.

I must also acknowledge the thoughtful help from my publisher, BookLogix in Alpharetta, Georgia, under their imprint of *Heavenly Light Press*. Their helpful suggestions especially about highlighting specific insights in larger print, in common use today, are appreciated.

And finally, it's a great delight to thank my most reliable, insightful and thoughtful editor – my talented, praying wife, Kay. Her practiced touch always makes better whatever I write.

Remember

Pray First,

Then Act!

Contents

Preface

None of us who pray faithfully and regularly can dare say we know all about prayer and praying. I suspect Deep Praying is all but unknowable this side of immortality. Yet, this Christ-follower wants to share a bit of what he's learned about praying so those who read this will gain at least a refreshed insight into this most high privilege of communicating with the God who made us, sustains us, redeems us, teaches us, and Who wants to bless us to be like His only begotten son, Jesus, our Christ.

Having read many fine books on praying, I believe I should share with you right here before you begin to read this book, what E.M. Bounds has said in one of his many writings on prayer. This one is entitled "Power Through Prayer", one of the Moody Classics published by them in 1979 and again in 2009. As you read his inspired and inspiring words, I hope you will see that the deeper and lasting results of praying to and with God is not some quick ten-minute, "Hi, how are you?" type of praying. Just as getting to know better a good friend of yours is accomplished by spending time with them, so it is with getting to know our great God. Here is the quote from E.M. Bounds.

Hurried devotions make weak faith, feeble convictions, questionable piety. To be little with God is to be little for God. To cut short the praying makes the whole religious character short, niggardly, and slovenly.

To pray is the greatest thing we can do; and to do it well there must be calmness, time, and deliberation; otherwise, it is degraded into the smallest and meanest of things. True praying has the largest results for good; and, poor praying, the least. We cannot do too much of real praying, we cannot do too little of the sham. We must learn anew the worth of prayer, enter anew the school of prayer.

None but praying leaders can have praying followers. Praying apostles will beget praying saints. A praying pulpit will beget praying pews. We do greatly need somebody who can set the saints to this business of praying. We are not a generation of praying saints. The greatest will he be of reformers and apostles, who can set the church to praying.

If you are willing to make the time available for such a marvelous thing, then do so. Some of you may be retired and can do so. Time alone with God is important. Give Him as much time as you are able. Even Jesus admonished Peter, His disciple, in the Garden, "Could you not watch with me even one hour?" (Mark 14:37).

My most profound objective for you in this study is **to rekindle your desire to spend more meaningful daily time with our Great Creator God by praying.** You will find yourself becoming victorious over those things that separate you from Him. I will try to stir your heart with His Love to the great power of believing Prayer – to renew (or establish) a vibrant relationship with God the Father, God the Son and God the Holy Spirit. And, yes, by so doing you will indeed bring Him glory. You will then continue on to enjoy Him more deeply all your life. A secondary objective is to prepare you to teach others so they, too, can have a victorious life in Christ.

All of this is so the church, to which we should each belong, will become a more worthy vessel for accomplishing what He calls us to do as a church. Perhaps, God will task you to help the leadership of your church restart an active praying ministry in the church.

Finally, let me say that this Study will mean little to you if you are not already a follower of Jesus Christ. So let me drop religious talk and instead talk facts – observed and proven historical facts about the life, death and resurrection from the dead of Jesus Christ.

The point? Jesus claimed He was (and still is) the only known Son of God. He made many wonderful claims and performed many awesome miracles to prove to the unbelieving and startled world that He was the Son of God. Many believed Him. Many scoffed. The religious and governmental powers decided He was a threat and must die. He was crucified in an agonizing death, laid in a tomb, only to rise to eternal life from that tomb in three days by the power of God His Father, as He had told His closest friends He would be. He was seen by hundreds over many days in His resurrected body. This enormously important fact is recorded in many written records of the time, not just in the Bible.

Conclusion? Only God can raise someone from the dead – so Jesus must have been exactly who He said He was – God in the flesh – come to earth to die to pay the penalty for the sins of you and me – so that each of us accepting this Fact, repenting of our wayward lives, and asking to be forgiven for our sins and their penalty, we can be accepted by God into His perfect Heaven with Him when we die here.

So now you have a choice to make. Those who accept the **facts** and ask Jesus to be their Savior from death to life, will enter Heaven upon their earthly death. Those who don't accept these **facts** and fail to turn their lives over to Jesus are doomed to enter eternal torment in Hell (John 3:36).

Let's be crystal clear. Christianity is not a religion – it is in fact a vibrant relationship with the living God – the same God who made you, loves you, sustains you, forgives you (if you repent), and teaches you. Never forget it – Christianity is a Relationship, not a Religion.

Let me suggest you Pray right now as you begin this study. Ask God to give you insights into His great gift of praying!

Chapter One
First Things First

Lehman Strauss, author in 1974 of "Sense and Nonsense About Prayer" says this in his Preface. *[There is] a condition which has existed in the church as long as I can remember and is growing increasingly worse. I refer to the low view of prayer.* He goes on to say he's *ministered in almost 1100 different churches across America and a common admission among too many professing Christians is an ineffective prayer life.* In my own experience, this has only grown worse since then.

Going on, he said, *There are two major weaknesses, as I view the situation. First, there is weakness in the pulpit ministry. Too many congregations are not getting sound, solid Bible teaching. The second weakness – a prayerless church – grows out of the first.*

He closes by saying, *It is my humble opinion that a return to the Biblical way of praying will bring spiritual power back to our lives and our churches.*

To that end, I have been moved by the Holy Spirit to write this concentrated study of insights on Praying. It began in late 2011 as a teaching manuscript; and was used to teach folks in my church and then pastors and church leaders in Mexico (Yucatan) in 2011. Lest you think I am setting myself up as an expert on the vast subject of praying, I am not. I am learning along with you. I have no doubt that God has called me to help the church to once again be a praying church. Your reading this indicates your genuine desire to strengthen the basics of praying. Here is what I have observed – as verified by Scripture...

Praying is to be a foundational activity of any Christ-follower and of any Church which is a Community of Faith in Almighty God through Jesus Christ!

It should fully engage us in the first of two basic activities of any Church (Acts 6:4). It is also listed elsewhere in Scripture as one of the four basic activities of any Church (Acts 2:42). It strikes me, then, that any church that does not pray regularly as the Body of Christ is out of line with His Word which may explain its weakness in addressing the Sinfulness of the culture around them.

The benefits of praying are many and rich.
Praying...

Enables us to experience the presence of God.

Encourages, strengthens and increases our Faith in God.

Brings His power into our challenges.

Helps us understand His Love more deeply.

Encourages joyful obedience to the Word of God.

Promotes Unity among church members.

Increases our desire and ability to pray effectively for personal and church spiritual growth.

Promotes a positive desire to share the Gospel as Christ commanded!

Develops a healthy determination to boldly influence the culture around us toward righteousness.

Develops a growing appetite for teaching on Prayer.

Promotes existing and new Prayer activities in the church.

And most important, it helps us know God more and more deeply.

All of which is to increase the intimacy of our walk with God, to empower us to share His love, and display an obedience that brings Him Glory. We receive spiritual power from Him through praying, especially when praying together with other Christ-followers. We evangelize more effectively by first praying for guidance and Holy Spirit power. We become stronger positive witnesses to the culture around us.

There are additional Benefits in Prayer Partnering (groups of two or three) in each Bible Fellowship Group:

To know each other better as we pray together.
To keep us focused and accountable to one another.
To knit us together as a functional part of God's active Family.
To mature us in our calling as disciple makers.

The Power of God is
invited into any situation
on the Wings of Prayer.
And all to the Praise of His Glory!

I hope this study will whet your appetite to continue your learning about this great **privilege of praying given us by our Creator God who invites us to speak with Him.** I urge you to use any of the excellent prayer resources listed in Enclosure One - Additional Reading.

Chapter Two
Praying Will Impact Our Lives

If you will allow it, the teachings of this study can grow you into a more Godly Christian, a more Holy Disciple. It is the escalating difference of going from **committed**, to **submitted**, to **surrendered**, to **abandoned to** becoming **His joyous bondservant!** Hopefully you're motivated to continue this journey.

If God is now only **present** in your life, or, better, **predominant** in your life, these teachings will help you elevate God to His rightful place of **preeminence** in your life. But you must allow the Holy Spirit of God (Who is in you if you are His) to use this teaching to do a mighty work in your heart of hearts to achieve this desirable end.

Why Is This Important?

When we spend frequent time with a friend, we each begin to take on characteristics of the other. Have you noticed that some long-married couples seem to have similar mannerisms and some even begin to look alike? In the very same way, as we spend more time conversing with our great God, over time we will begin to absorb and reflect His character and characteristics. We become more like Him as we spend time with Him.

Focal Verses: I hope these verses have special meaning as we begin this journey.

Jeremiah 29:11-13 – *For I know the plans I have for you, says the Lord. They are plans for good and not for disaster, to give you a future and a hope. In those days when you pray, I will listen. If you look for me wholeheartedly, you will find me.*

Matthew 6:6-15, 25-34; 7:7-11; 18-20 – *But when you pray, go away by yourself, shut the door behind you, and pray to your Father in private. Then your Father, who sees everything, will reward you. When you pray, don't babble on and on as other religions do. They think their prayers are answered merely by repeating their words again and again. Don't be like them, for your Father knows exactly what you need even before you ask him! Pray like this: Our Father in heaven, may your name be kept holy. May your Kingdom come soon. May your will be done on earth, as it is in heaven. Give us today the food we need, and forgive us our sins, as we have forgiven those who sin against us. And don't let us yield to temptation; but, rescue us from the evil one. If you forgive those who sin against you, your heavenly Father will forgive you. But if you refuse to forgive others, your Father will not forgive your sins. That is why I tell you not to worry about everyday life – whether you have enough food and drink, or enough clothes to wear. Isn't life more than food and your body more than clothing? Look at the birds. They don't plant or harvest or store food in barns, for your heavenly Father feeds them. And aren't you far more valuable to him than they are: Can all your worries add a single moment to your life? And why worry about your clothing? Look at the lilies of the field and how they grow. They don't work or make their clothing, yet Solomon in all his glory was not dressed as beautifully as they are. And if God cares so wonderfully for wildflowers that are here today and thrown into the fire tomorrow, he will certainly care for you. Why do you have so little faith? So don't worry about these things, saying 'What will we eat? What will we drink? What will we wear? These things dominate the thoughts of unbelievers, but your heavenly Father already knows all your needs.* ***Seek the Kingdom of God above all else, and live righteously, and he will give you everything you need.*** *So, don't worry about tomorrow, for tomorrow will bring its own worries. Today's trouble is enough for today.*

Keep on asking, and you will receive what you ask for. Keep on seeking, and you will find. Keep on knocking, and the door will be opened to you. For everyone who asks, receives. Everyone who seeks, finds. And to everyone who knocks, the door will be opened. You parents – if your children ask for a loaf of bread, do you give them a stone instead? Or if they ask for a fish, do you give them a snake? Of course not! So if you sinful people know how to give good gifts to your children, ***how much more will your heavenly Father give good gifts to those who ask him.***

A good tree can't produce bad fruit, and a bad tree cannot produce good fruit. So every tree that does not produce good fruit is chopped down and thrown into the fire. Yes, just as you can identify a tree by its fruit, so you can identify people by their actions. So pray often with our great and awesome God who made us and Loves us.

I Timothy 2:1-4 – *I urge you, first of all, to pray for all people. Ask God to help them; intercede on their behalf, and give thanks for them. Pray this way for kings and all who are in authority so that we can live peaceful and quiet lives marked by godliness and dignity.* ***This is good and pleases God our Savior, who wants everyone to be saved and to understand the truth.***

James 5:16 – *Confess your sins to each other and pray for each other so that you may be healed.* ***The earnest prayer of a righteous person has great power and produces wonderful results.***

Revelation 8:3-4 – *Then another angel with a gold incense burner came and stood at the altar. And a great amount of incense was given to him* ***to mix with the prayers of God's people as an offering on the gold altar before the throne. The smoke of the incense, mixed with prayers of God's holy people, ascended up to God from the altar where the angel had poured them out.***

Chapter Three
The Purpose of Praying

The Westminster (Shorter) catechism answers the question: "What is the chief end of man?" with this answer: "Man's chief end is to Glorify God and enjoy Him forever." Without praying, that would be impossible... I hope you will see that praying – mighty prevailing, believing praying – by followers of Christ, must be the undergirding and animating dynamic for all the other activities of God's church. Without it, the others begin to wither – or worse – begin to be done only in man's strength. This may be one of the primary reasons so many churches are dying or are becoming secular or apostate.

Boiling it all down, what are the fundamental reasons we are invited by our life-giving and life-saving God to speak with Him – our truly awe-inspiring, Holy God?

The **first reason** should be the most obvious: To grow **to know our Almighty God** as Father, Son and Holy Spirit better, much better! Knowing His will and experiencing His Amazing Holiness, more and more deeply, is worth every minute spent with Him in abandonment of self.

Praying describes the unique communication of a human being with his creator God – who *is* the only God in all the universe. As we know, there are other gods conjured up by the mind of man, but none of those gods are the creator God of heaven, earth and all the universe. To know God is to spend time with Him – in praying and in reading His book, the Holy Bible with contemplation and understanding. None of us can truly know someone unless we spend time with them. The more time spent deepens the knowing.

The **second reason** may not be so obvious, but it may truly be the reason why God wants to talk with us. He wants to share His wisdom with us **so that we come to examine and know**

ourselves better – to listen attentively and acceptingly to Him as He transforms us to become more like our Savior Jesus Christ, who **is** our Almighty Lord God! Do not be put off or become discouraged when He sends difficult circumstances to get your attention; it's to drive you to listen to Him. Stop and truly **listen**! He does speak to us as we wait upon Him in searching silence – a small, still voice in our minds.

Because God made you and loves you as your Heavenly Father, he wants contact with you, as does any parent with their child. He wants you to know Him and He wants to teach you right from wrong, as does any loving parent for their child. He has given us a book, the His-story book of right and wrong lessons, and of wisdom. That ageless* book, His Holy Bible, is the second way He speaks to us to help us along life's rough road toward Him! It drives us to confess our sins and repent; to strive to do better.

> * "Ageless" is used quite accurately and simply because the heart of man from the first man, Adam, to each of us today, is the same *desperately wicked* heart. The Bible is Truth eternal and applies to each member of the human race.

And there is a **third reason** for praying with God: **To intercede and lift others before God** for salvation, healing, direction...and to ask Him for what we need, or think we need. Asking for what we need, when we've broken relationship with our God, is poignantly but beautifully modeled for us by King David in his Psalm 51, verses ten through thirteen:

Create in me a clean heart, O God.
Renew a right spirit within me.
Do not banish me from your presence,
and don't take your Holy Spirit from me
Restore me to the joy of your salvation,
and make me willing to obey you.
Then I will teach your ways to rebels,
and they will return to you.

Worship Pastor Larry Harrison of Crossings Community Church in Oklahoma City says of this passage: *Only God can do what David asks, to give a clean heart. And the request isn't to take the old, tainted heart and restore it. The request is for a brand new, never-been-used-before heart. It's that place within each of us where we meet with God. Once you have a clean heart, the rest of the Psalm is possible: to renew a right spirit, to restore joy, and to be used once again and be effective for His glory.*

We pray
to examine and know ourselves better
to listen attentively and acceptingly
to Him as He transforms us!

In Paul David Tripp's book "New Morning Mercies" (Crossway, 2014) he writes provocatively in his April 30 devotion about a seldom considered aspect of praying.

> *Praying is an act of worship. Praying is an act of submission. Praying is an act of obedience. But praying is also an act of admission. Every instance of praying is a confession in which I own my condition and embrace my need. Praying that doesn't do this may be a religious recitation of some sort, but it ceases to be praying. In praying, I confess once again that I won't ever be what I'm supposed to be and do what I am supposed to do without the forgiving, empowering, and delivering grace of the One to whom I am praying. Praying decimates my independent self-surety; it puts my utter dependency before my eyes and calls me to cry out for the help that I am so often tempted to deny I need.*
>
> *To reduce praying to a grocery list of things that you want and think you need not only demeans praying, but it also demeans the sacrifice of love*

that the one to whom you are praying made so that you and your prayers would be received. The heart of true praying is vertical confession, not horizontal desire.

Self-righteousness crushes praying, reducing it to an empty religious recitation spoken by one who sees himself as a grace graduate. Run to Jesus in your poverty and weakness, and know that he is never revolted when you do, but always greets you with arms of grace.

I've listed below some of the excellent scriptures that speak to the issue of praying and why we should. I suggest you look each of them up in your Bible to become familiar with where they are and to know precisely what each one says.

To repent and ask for forgiveness (1 John 1:9)

To acknowledge His righteousness and awesome Holiness (Exodus 3:5; Is 6:3, Luke 5:8; 1 Kings 18:36,37)

To acknowledge His mercy (Psalm 103:8-12)

To enjoy His Presence (Psalm 46:10; 112)

To praise and worship Him for Who He is (Psalm 100; 111; 145)

To be quiet and listen to God tell you what is on His Mind (Psalm 25:4,5)

To thank God for what He is doing and has done for you (Hebrews 13:15; John 15:5)

To petition God for self or others (Matthew 7:7-11; Exodus 33:13; 1 John 5:14,15)

To ask God to tell you what you are to do (Psalm 143:8,10; Jeremiah 29:11-13)

To let God know you are upset (Job 30:20,21)

To let the Holy Spirit speak of your deep needs and His will (Romans 8:26,27)

And one of my all-time favorites is Psalms 37:4 "Take delight in the Lord and He will give you your heart's desires." When I was a new Christian, I saw that verse and immediately, because I liked sailing, thought that if I grew much closer to God and delighted myself in Him, He would enable me to buy the 44-foot Pilot House Ketch to be properly outfitted for a long-desired sailing trip around the world. As I grew closer and closer to God in my daily times for praying, I noticed that my desire for that sailboat became less and less, and my desire to be more involved in Bible Study and Teaching, and in talking with others about Him. In other words, delighting myself in Him changed my heart's desire from my want to His wants. How utterly amazing is His Grace! And I couldn't be happier about that extraordinary outcome!

Dr. Strauss makes it quite clear.

> *We Christians cannot afford to neglect a quiet time alone with God at the beginning of each day. The servant is not greater than his Lord. If our lives and our efforts are to bring forth fruit that will remain, we need divine direction every day. If we make our plans ahead, let them be made only after we have prayed for God's leading. And even then, we must come daily to Him, because He might change our plans.* [But more to the point, we <u>need</u> His guidance daily.] *Our sphere of activity for each new day must* [should] *be preceded by prayer, so as to allow the Holy Spirit to choose for us. Just as our Savior would not choose His own program without first praying to*

the Father, neither should we. It is not possible for a Christian to know God's best for him apart from prayer.

Christians cannot afford to neglect a Quiet Time alone with God at the beginning of each day!

Let me use another of the marvelous insights from Paul David Tripp's book "New Morning Mercies" (Crossway, 2014):

"Praying is abandoning your place in the center of your world and daily surrendering that place to God alone as an act of heartfelt worship.

Praying is much more than bringing to God your list of wants, desires, and needs.

It is a radical act of worship that reminds you of who you are, who God is, and what life is all about. ***Praying is surrender***

1. *It's surrender to the reality that there is someone more ultimate than you.*
2. *It's surrender to the reality that life isn't just about you.*
3. *It's surrender to the reality that you need help.*
4. *It's surrender to the reality that there is wisdom greater than yours.*
5. *It's surrender of your right to live as you choose.*
6. *It's surrender of your hopes to God's grace.*

So [when you] close your eyes, bow your head, and surrender – be thankful for the grace that meets you as you do."

A brief word about the types of Praying:

Personal or Private Praying is the category of prayer we are most familiar with because it is the type we most often practice – or should practice. Another category of praying is Group Praying; it also goes by the names of "corporate" or "communal" or "united".

In each of these categories, Personal or Group, we may Praise God, Worship God, Petition God for our needs and/or the needs of others (intercession), Thank God, and Confess/Repent to God.

At Enclosure Two, I've included an instructive paper to further your knowledge about Intercession. Also, the special "rules" of engagement or protocols, if you will, for group praying are presented in Chapter Six as paragraphs two and three under "Sense and Nonsense."

Conversational Praying (Enclosure 4) is an additional guide for a method of structured praying for group use that came back into vogue in the early 1970s. I strongly recommend you teach this type of group praying because it is naturally how we converse with each other and, I believe, it's the way God Himself most enjoys conversing with us, based on Old Testament examples, especially with Moses.

One additional thought on types of praying. Usually when we pray in groups, we use a mode of prayer called "agreement" or sequential prayer. Only one person prays at a time, with others periodically "agreeing" by saying things like "amen" or "yes, Lord" and similar (this is an excellent way to encourage each other as we pray). There is also a mode known as "concert" of prayer. That is, as its name implies, when all pray aloud at once. This is seldom used in collocated groups but is used widely in prayer movements across a region or nation when people in different locations all pray on a topic simultaneously at the same time. I tell you this simply to make you aware of these types of praying.

Chapter Four
The Power in Praying

Many believers say there is power in Praying. It is commonly said, but is it true? **Actually, there is NOT power in *our* prayer. The POWER is in God's resounding answers to our prayer.** His is the Kingdom, the Power and the Glory, and we are only tapping into His power by praying in His will. "For God is working in you, giving you the desire and **power** to do what pleases Him." (Philippians 2:13)

Let me illustrate this: visualize a table lamp. By itself, there is no power in it. You must plug into a power source first. Even then the lamp will not light up; it has to be switched on. Similarly, a human is "lifeless" (dead in trespasses and sin) until saved. Then the Holy Spirit of God indwells us in the power of God. But you cannot access that power and "light" up your life without praying, which is our switch to the "on" position. **By praying in the Spirit we tap into the power of God**. When we do pray in the Spirit (Ephesians 6:18) we are indeed praying with Power – **His Power**.

If, however, we pray in the flesh, we are praying without God's Power. Fleshly prayers are also known as "soulish" prayers; they are insincere and meant to impress either God or others who can hear you. Either way, they are prayers "dead on arrival".

Let me refer you to six excellent examples of this power of God in Answered Prayer. These are from "The Praying Church Source Book", 2nd Edition, CRC Pubs. You may order copies of this book from Faith Alive at this address: https://www.faithaliveresources.org/Products/216850/the-praying-church-sourcebook.aspx.

1) Mother/Daughter/Christ, page 241. Tells the story of the result of a Mother's praying for her daughter's salvation.
2. Angels Watching over Me, page 242. An exciting miracle story of an Indian evangelist to Tibet.
3. Prayer through the Ages. Page 242. Fourteen examples from the Bible of God reliably answering Prayer.
4. George Müller. Page 243. A must read to see how God answers persistent prayer.
5. Even the Little Things. Page 243. Shows God's interest in "even the little things".
6. Supernatural "Greenbacks". Page 244. God is interested even in our money at times.

Though the power in our praying is not our power but is the power of the Holy Spirit in us, **there IS power in our Faith to Pray Expectantly because our Faith is in Him Who is the all-powerful God of the impossible.** We know He can do all in His Will that we ask or think, and much more beyond – but we must Pray Believing. And since all Faith comes from God to us, if you believe your Faith to be too small, then your first prayer may need to be, **"God, I believe, but help my unbelief, help my weak Faith to grow to believe your will to do what is needed."**

* *

"The Prayer for Healing"

By Jon Graf, President of Church Prayer Leader's Network
Should be a High Priority and Shows the Power of God!

> *Back in my childhood, I remember that every communion Sunday we had a time where people could come forward for prayer for healing. Following the command in James, Elders would ask if they had sin to confess, anoint them with oil, and pray for Christ to heal. I even remember some who were healed instantly.*

Somewhere along the line, most churches have stopped that practice in services. A good number, however, would do it privately if a person asks. But people do not ask, because it is never mentioned to do so. It is almost exclusively only practiced in Pentecostal churches who believe (per Isaiah 53:5 and 1 Peter 2:24) that healing is also included in the Atonement (a belief I personally hold, as do many non-Pentecostal churches as well). Yet it used to be practiced in many streams of the church. What happened?

In the West, it was probably the explosion of knowledge and availability of services in modern medicine that caused people to ask for the elders to anoint with oil, less and less. But skepticism and the lack of churches regularly making prayer for healing available (except for putting the request on a prayer list or chain) has certainly been a culprit as well.

The result is that while every believer would likely say they believe God has the power to heal, few think He will heal in most situations. Or if He does, it will primarily be through "His giving knowledge to" doctors and the right medicine.

Revive the Practice

Whatever the reason, we will not see many testimonies of miraculous healing if we give only mild lip service to pray for healing! We need to make prayer for healing visible again on Sunday mornings. We need to teach on faith (though only a small amount needed by the asker) and on expectation. If we and our people have no sense of expectation that God will move in a church service or as we pray for healing, He very likely will not move!

Recently in the church where I am preaching, I did a 3-week series on healing. Multiple times I talked about expectation. When we gave people a chance to be anointed and prayed for, I was stunned by the significant response! In the days that followed I received more texts and email comments from people thanking me for the emphasis than I did any other message.

Every Thursday night for the last two years in June and July, events called "Jesus Rallies" have been held in the little town of Ephrata, PA (Lancaster County). Led by Circuit Rider GenZer, Joel Bomberger, these worship and preaching events have seen 800-1000 people every week, dozens saved and baptized each week, and many miraculous instantaneous healings, including spines straightening, and several girls' cutter scars on arms disappearing in front of the individual as prayer for healing was offered. (Needless to say, the girls surrendered their lives to Jesus and booked it to the baptismal tank!)

In these days, we need to raise our level of expectation for healing and make the practice of praying for healing both often and visible again!

* *

One more insight on the issue of Power in Praying, let me remind you that there are several places in our Holy Bible, where we are told specifically to take authority from God into our hands and use it against the devil, the evil one. One such place is in James 4:7,8. It reads like this: ***So humble yourselves before God. Resist the devil, and he will flee from you. Come close to God, and God will come close to you***. Here God has deliberately given us authority and power to resist the devil and tell him, in the name and authority of God, to get out and to take his malady or infirmity with him – to flee from you... Hallelujah!!!

I am praying to You because
I know You will answer, O God.
Bend down and Listen as I pray.
Psalm 17:6

Chapter Five
The Priority of Praying

As mentioned earlier about the proper priority of praying in a believer's life, the Book of Acts of the Apostles has the definitive answer in verse 42 of Chapter 2, *They were continually devoting themselves to the apostles'* ***teaching****, and to* ***fellowship****, to the* ***breaking of bread****, and to* ***PRAYER***. So, there it is. Praying is one of the four basic activities of the church, any Christ-centered church. **Teaching** is the bedrock of any church; without it there is no understanding. **Fellowship** is one of the foundation blocks also; without it there is no partnership or sharing which is vital to any organization. **Breaking of Bread** refers to fellowshipping together around a good meal as well as to the Lord's Supper or Communion; without it, there is incomplete reverence and worship of God for Who He is and what He did to found the Church. Finally, there is **Prayer** (or better, **Praying**) as one of the founding four Pillars of the Church; **without it there is no spiritual growth and no real fellowship with our Almighty God.**

Look also at Acts 6:4 "*Then we apostles* [Elders, today] *can spend our time in* ***Prayer*** *and teaching the word*." It is clear that praying is, or should be, one of the two most important activities of leaders and members of any church.

Perhaps the clearest indication in all of God's Word about the priority of Praying, is stated emphatically by Jesus Christ Himself in each of the Gospels. (Matthew 21:13, Mark 11:17 and Luke 19:46) They each say the following or similar, "My temple shall be a house of Prayer for all nations." And that top priority has been so even back in the Old Testament era; Read Isaiah 56:7 to confirm it for yourself. Our only conclusion must be that to the God who created us, praying to Him must be of paramount importance, a top priority! Is it for you? If not, then does this help you see how important to your entire life that praying is? We hope so...

Praying is or should be a principal foundation of any Church. Without it there is no spiritual growth and no fellowship with our Holy God.

While pondering late at night how to articulate the importance of praying in our spiritual life, I believe God gave me an analogy. Picture in your mind a column of words under the title "BODY". Arrayed under that would be three words: FOOD, DRINK, and BREATH. Now, envision another column headed by the title, "SPIRIT". What word would you put opposite FOOD in this SPIRIT column? How about THE WORD or BREAD OF LIFE? What word would you put opposite "DRINK" in this "SPIRIT" column? How about PRAISE or WORSHIP? And, finally, what word would you put in the "SPIRIT" column opposite "BREATH"? How about "PRAYING"? What's the point?

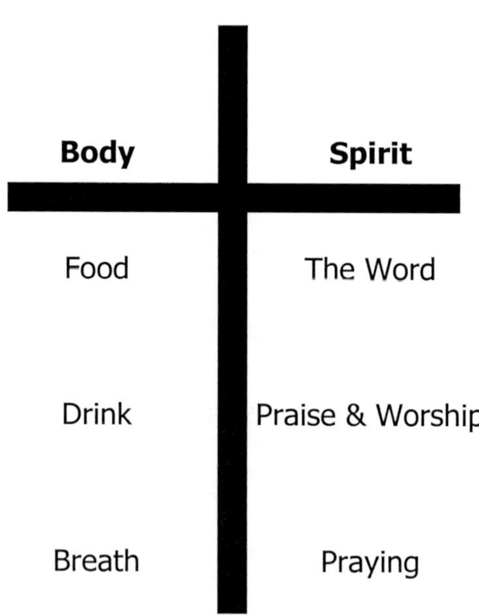

Our bodies can live for weeks without food, for days without water, but only minutes without breath. And, if you are a Christian, so it is with our spiritual selves: you can survive spiritually without reading the Word for a while, but you won't thrive. Without Worshipping and Praising God, most of us will get by again, but only for a while; our souls yearn to worship God and if we don't, we begin to shrivel spiritually. But without prayer and confession, without communing with God regularly, you will quite literally begin to die spiritually. A Christian who lives without praying will walk about with little or no evidence of the Holy Spirit of God in him. Without breath, our bodies become quickly brain dead and then the body dies. Without praying, our spirit loses touch with the Holy Spirit of God, and we become "heart" dead or spiritually dead, followed by hypocrisy in our behavior. Praying keeps us real and vibrant for God's use in the lives of others. And we depend on wisdom from God's Spirit, which we gain from spending time with Him through praying (and reading His Word).

Praying keeps us real and vibrant for God's use in the lives of others.

Let's take a look at what "The Battle Plan for Prayer" by Stephen & Alex Kendrick has to say about "The Priority of Praying":

> *God has strategically chosen to establish and utilize prayer as part of His sovereign plan for us. It is like oxygen to our spiritual lives. It provides the needed wind in our sails to propel everything we do as believers, and it's the unseen key to the success of every ministry of the church.*
>
> *It allows God's children to interact with our heavenly Father like beloved sons and daughters before their earthly father (Matthew 7:9-11). Prayer aligns the body of Christ with her Head. It's the key to intimacy between the bride of*

Christ and her Bridegroom. Human frailty, joined in communion with divine perfection. Prayer is simply too wonderful and important not to do it. It's a big deal to God and should be a big deal to us.

But praying isn't always easy. It can feel very counter-intuitive to pause when we have so much to do, trying to focus our thoughts in the midst of a million distractions, say no to our selfishness and self-sufficiency, and humble ourselves before an Almighty God whom we cannot control and cannot presently see or hear with our physical senses. It seems easier just to go out and attempt to fix things ourselves than to stop and pray about them. So we tend to put it off and save it as an emergency parachute during times of crisis.

But approaching a holy and sovereign God in prayer is something we should prize and never take for granted. We are very needy of God. He created the universe from nothing by the power of His spoken word. We, on the other hand, have never created anything. He is perfect and maintains all authority in heaven and earth, while we stumble in many ways (Luke 9:23; James 3:2). God is dependent on nothing at all while we are completely dependent on Him every second of every day (John15:4,5). He knows every detail of everything in all places at all times (Psalm139:1-18), while we don't know what will happen tomorrow and are already forgetting what we did yesterday.

That is why prayer [or praying] should be first in the order of things *(1 Tim 2:1-8).*

Let me share with you a short story about praying. Many years ago when I was teaching a middle school Sunday School class, I hit upon an idea about praying that resonated with them. I simply said that when they get up each morning, start their day by praying to God. But I suggested they pretend they are taking their phone off the hook (back before cell phones) to make that morning prayer call to God. And, I said, when you are finished that prayer, pretend not to "hang up" but simply "leave the phone off the hook". Then during the day if you want to talk to God, simply speak to Him because you are already still connected with Him by leaving your prayer phone "off the hook". The concept of knowing you are always able to immediately reach up in prayer to our great God no matter where you are is freeing – and comforting. But to open the channel for the day, start praying when you get up every morning.

What is Praying's Priority in your life?

Think on these...

How big is your God?

What is your perception of Him?

Is that a limitation on your faith in praying?

Judging by your time spent praying, is it important to you?

What are your *real* hindrances to talking with God regularly?

How deep is your intimacy with God through praying?

Does temptation become a serious tormentor when your praying is stagnant and atrophied? (1 Corinthians 10:13)

Is Praying a Mystery for you?

One of the first things we should do is to dispel right up front the notion that praying is a mystery. Is speaking with your spouse a mystery? Is speaking with a good friend a mystery? Is speaking with your boss a mystery? Is speaking with anyone a mystery? Then why should we ever consider speaking with God a mystery? To be sure He is God Almighty, but He invites us to speak with Him. He has given us speech and He has spoken with several of the Old Testament people. Speech is not some grand and mysterious thing. When spoken by a prophet, saint or other person, speech is straightforward, though certainly (in most cases) respectful, even deferential. And when God spoke to some of them, He was straightforward, direct and usually brief.

This quote is the Study Note on Psalm 4:3 of the NLT Life Application Bible:

> *Sometimes we think that God will not hear us because we have fallen short of His high standards for Holy Living. But if we have trusted Christ for salvation, God has forgiven us and He will listen to us. When you feel as though your prayers are bouncing off the ceiling, remember that as a believer you have been set apart by God and that He loves you.* ***He hears and answers although His answers may not be what you expect. Look at your problems in the light of God's power instead of looking at God in the shadow of your problems.***

So then, let us forever dispel any idea that praying is somehow to be anything more than respectful conversation by any one of us humbled Christians with our great and awesome God. As one man was quoted as saying, "Do you think God is impressed if you speak to Him as though you were a Shakespearian actor with a steeple stuck in your throat?" He wants us to be ourselves though quite mindful of Who He is and who we are. Remember that the purpose of praying is to communicate with God. **Being respectfully conversational is all that is needed.**

But let's be honest about this. There is one aspect of praying that is a mystery to most of us. And that is the mystery of God's response to our petitions. And thus will it ever be, unless and until we know God's will perfectly and pray that way.

Look at your problems
in the light of God's power
instead of looking at God
in the shadow of your problems.

To Whom do we Pray?

When Jesus answered his disciples' request to teach them to pray, He said, "Pray, then, in this way: 'Our Father, Who is in heaven.'" You might say, then, that we are to pray ONLY to the Father. But then, aren't Jesus and the Holy Spirit of God also God? Yes, they are. Is it wrong to pray to Jesus? No. Is it wrong to pray to the Holy Spirit of God, Who, by the way, is in you (if you are a Christ-follower)? No. Is it wrong to pray to any person outside the Godhead. I would say, yes, on the strength that only the Trinity of God the Father, God the Son, and God the Holy Spirit is God.

Another way to clarify this sometimes-difficult issue is to remember "where" each of these God-persons is. God the Father is thought to be in His heaven – yet, we know He is omnipresent, so He can be anywhere in Heaven or Creation that He cares to be, or be everywhere at once. Jesus is seated at the right hand of the throne of God the Father, ever interceding on our behalf. And the Holy Spirit is in each Christ-follower as the helper and comforter Whom Jesus said He would send us after He returned to the Father in Heaven. So, because they are all in perfect communication with each other at all times, you may pray to any of them. For myself, I tend to go with Jesus' example to pray to the Father, and, when making a petition, to ask it in the name of His Son Jesus, as Jesus instructed us. But I do pray to the Holy Spirit, too, as the issue may dictate. Incidentally, it makes no good sense to close any prayer with "in the name of Jesus" unless it is truly a petition prayer.

Chapter Six
Hindrances to God Hearing My Praying

The thirteen topic headings are from the first thirteen chapters of Dr Lehman Strauss' book, "Sense and Nonsense About Prayer."

With the exception of a few quoted sections, I have used my words to shorten each of the chapters. But the thoughts are all Dr Strauss's; I use them because I want you to have their wisdom.

I believe you will determine you had no idea there were so many hindrances or stumbling blocks to effective praying. By effective praying I mean praying prayers that God hears and answers. But let me quickly add that there is an antidote to these "hindrances" to effective praying. Of course, it is to **confess, repent and to ask forgiveness for allowing one or more of these "hindrances" into your life** (1 Jn 1:9).

And that means that **you must be aware of these** so that when they crop up in your life, you will deal with them immediately and correctly.

Sense or Nonsense?

Speak to God as the highly intelligent being He is. Have you ever listened to others as they pray? Some people think they should sound like some high theologian academic. Some sound like stained-glass windows. Many are really incoherent. Often people will use the Lord's title every few words. Some will even **preach to God** from His own Word – as though He hadn't ever heard it before. Some will endlessly use the expression, "Lord, we know thus and so..." as though God did not know that you knew that. Others insert the word "just" in almost every sentence, "Lord, we just love You" or "just want such-and-such."

Some will thoughtlessly, in group praying, pray on and on about all manner of issues – completely heedless of the fact there are others present who need to raise their voices to God, if only for an instant. Lengthy personal prayer in a group setting suggests that you are really impressed with either the sound of your own voice or, worse, how well you think you pray – or that you are not even thinking of others (Matthew 6:7). Group Praying is different from personal prayer.

One way to break this bad habit is to begin to pray in private in shorter "bursts" – one issue and only a few sentences at a time. Why? So you give God time to respond to what you've already prayed. The same applies when you pray with your spouse, for the same reason. Thus retrained, you are now properly fitted to enter responsible group praying. No one, especially God, likes someone who "multiplies his words" (Job 35:16).

Praying and Unconfessed Sin

Does it make sense to ask anything of God if there is unconfessed sin in your heart? This is one of the surest ways to prevent God from hearing or answering your prayer. (Psalm 66:18; Isaiah 59:1,2; 1:13-15; Psalm 24:3,4)

God hates sham and hypocrisy – especially so in worship and praying, presumably.

(Isaiah 1:16). But if we are swift to keep short accounts with God (Proverb 28:13), we retain our sweet fellowship with Him and can receive His blessings and mercy.

Humble yourself before our Almighty God (Job 22:29; Psalm 25:9). Read also what Daniel prayed in Daniel 9:4,5. James also in chapter five, verse 16 of his great letter made it clear we are to be emptied out and wholly surrendered – to be heard and blessed by God, "The effective praying of a righteous man can accomplish much." (James 5:16b)

To pray when we are in sin is powerless praying. It is worthless. By sins, we are talking about not only the great, gross sins of immorality, but also those listed in Ephesians 4:25-32;

5:3-5. Sin, great or small, causes God to view the sinner as having committed all of these (James 2:10).

"If we confess our sins, God is faithful and righteous to forgive us our sins, and to cleanse us from all unrighteousness." (1 John 1:9). Frankly, we should all begin our praying by confessing we are sinners and ask him to cleanse us of all unrighteousness. Then, having a pure heart and clean hands we are welcome to ascend up to God in prayer (Psalm 24:3,4)

Praying and Selfishness

"You ask and do not receive, because you ask with wrong motives, (literally: wickedly), so that you may spend it on your pleasures." (James 4:3) Sincerity and a spirit of worship are NOT sufficient to make up a valid petition if my motive is selfish. Ask yourself, "Is there pretense in my motive for asking?"

Better is verse 4 of Psalm 37 "Delight yourself in the Lord, and He will give you the desires of your heart." Oh, but there is real danger in misinterpreting this treasured verse. What do you think it means? Consider this: If you are truly delighting yourself in the Lord, then you are thinking like Him – and so, your desires at that point are in complete agreement with His desires for you. So it's not about getting what you want, but about getting what He wants you to have. Perhaps this verse is best understood through the lens of Matthew 6:33, "But seek first His Kingdom and His Righteousness and all these things* will be added to you." *(food, drink, clothing, shelter, etc.)

Self-examination is very important. It makes sense to examine our motives before we ask anything of God. So – put God's Kingdom concerns first – and He will bless you – when you ask, seek and knock. (Matthew 7:7)

Praying and the Holy Spirit

It makes no sense to pray if we do not pray in the Spirit. Ephesians 6:18 makes it quite clear: *"With all prayer and petition pray at all times in the Spirit..."* *"One of the truly great secrets of a successful prayer life,"* Lehman Straus claimed, *"was to pray in the Holy Spirit."*

Real praying is spiritual warfare. We Christians are in a conflict, and praying is our mighty weapon. **But we must view praying not as a ritual but as a relationship with the Holy Spirit.** The spiritual weakness that plagues most of us grows out of our failure to enter into that experience which Paul called "the communion of the Holy Spirit" (2 Cor 13:14).

How do we bring this excellent knowledge into our praying practice?

> **First**, we need to know – really know and practice – that the Holy Spirit dwells in us. "Do you not know that you are a temple of God and that the Spirit of God dwells in you?" (1 Cor 3:16).
>
> **Second**, we can ask the Holy Spirit to pray for us when we know not what to pray in a particular situation. Be familiar with the verses in Romans 8:26,27 that say, "In the same way the Spirit also helps our weakness, for we do not know how to pray as we should, but the Spirit Himself intercedes for us with groanings too deep for words; and He who searches the hearts knows what the mind of the Spirit is, because He intercedes for the saints according to the will of God." In short, the Holy Spirit assists us in our praying by giving to us the right desire and direction.
>
> **Third**, we must be careful to not grieve the Holy Spirit (Eph 4:30). What are some of the ways we can grieve the Spirit? By lying, anger, stealing,

dirty and useless conversations, malice, unkindness, and so forth. In short, **any sin grieves the Spirit**. By grieving the Holy Spirit, we cannot enlist His help – and we must have His help if our prayers are to be effective. We can do even more damage to our relationship with the Holy Spirit by continued disobedience and sin. We can "quench" the Spirit (1Thessalonians 5:19).

Fourth, we must be filled with the Holy Spirit to overflowing, as we are instructed to be in Ephesians 6:18. Being filled simply means being controlled by the Spirit; that is, your mind and will are abandoned to His control. We surrender our will to His. We invite Him in to minister to us as we seek God in prayer. Some of the toughest praying is done in the Spirit, because it is in those times when the issues seem so large and difficult that we don't really know how to pray. If we cultivate praying in the Spirit, it will bring about a change in our prayer life which we hardly thought possible.

It makes no sense to pray
if we do not pray in the Spirit.

Praying in Jesus' Name

The person who holds a light view of the Lord Jesus Christ cannot have a worthwhile prayer life. Jesus Himself told us to pray in His name for those things we ask; see John 14:13,14 and again John 16:23,24,26.

And then there is the most awesome of verses, John 14:6, where Christ Jesus said, "I am the Way, the Truth, and the Life; no one comes to the Father but through Me." It is clear. No man can come to the Father unless he has come to Jesus first. He who rejects the Son has no access to the Father.

This statement by Jesus is usually taken to mean that we can come to God for Justification (Salvation) only by accepting Jesus' sacrifice on the cross as full and sufficient payment for the penalty for our sins. And that is true. But there is the other meaning; you cannot come to God in prayer if you have not accepted Christ as your Lord and Savior. A small point, you say? Not so. It is a major point in anyone's praying life. If you are not in Christ, you do not have the Holy Spirit residing in you; without the Holy Spirit you can have no hearing of your praying, as discussed in the previous section – except, of course, the cry of a broken and contrite heart for Jesus' forgiveness and salvation.

To pray in Christ's name is to pray in union and communion with Christ Himself. It is not using His name as a magic formula to get what I want, but as a means of honoring and glorifying Him. The name of Jesus is the authority that opens the door into God's presence and gives us the right to be heard. God is not obliged to give audience to any person who does not regard and respect His Son. One of the good things about trusting Christ and glorifying Him is that it puts us on praying ground, so that we may call upon God at any time. It is powerless and unprevailing praying that omits the name of our Lord Jesus Christ!

God is Light. Those without the Light are in darkness. The Light can have nothing to do with darkness. And since prayer is communion with God, only those in the light can be heard in prayer. Therefore regular communion with God, who is light, can only be "enjoyed" by those who are in the light – that is, those who have received Jesus as Savior. If you are in darkness, it is impossible to have communion in prayer with God. (2 Cor 6:14).

Praying and Faith

It does not make sense to pray without Faith. To know God is to trust Him. The faith that is essential to prayer is always faith in God. When we pray, we do not need confidence in ourselves nor in our prayers, but in God.

"And without faith it is impossible to please Him, for he who comes to God must believe that He is and that He is a rewarder of those who seek Him." (Heb 11:6) Faith is here declared to involve belief in a Person. Show me a man who believes God, and you have shown me a man who prays.

We all know of the great Faith chapter in the Bible, Hebrews chapter 11. Verse one says, "Now faith is the assurance of things hoped for, the conviction of things not seen." Faith takes the promise of God and says, "I am confident that it will be exactly as God said it will be, because I have confidence in God."

Dr Strauss says, *My belief in the possibility of prayer is based upon the doctrine of God. Because I believe in God's omniscience, omnipotence, and faithfulness, I can depend on Him. Only the person who knows and trusts in God, and who has asked of Him and received, has proved the objective value of prayer. If you tell me God does not answer prayer, I will write you off as a person who either does not know God, or does not trust Him, or both. Discover the God of the Bible, place full confidence in Him, and then you will begin to learn how to ask and receive. While I cannot comprehend God fully, I know that He has perfect knowledge and unlimited power, and that He loves me and is concerned for my welfare; therefore, I will trust Him.*

To waver is to doubt. If you have any doubts about God, why pray? If you want your faith increased, do as the apostles did in Luke 17:5: ask the Lord to increase your faith.

Praying and Unforgiveness

For the same reason that it is impossible for God to hear my prayer if I have unconfessed sin in my heart, it is impossible for Him to hear my prayers if I have regarded Unforgiveness in my heart. In fact, an unforgiving heart is one of the unconfessed sins, isn't it?

In Mark 11:25, Jesus tells His disciples, "Whenever you stand praying, forgive, if you have anything against anyone, so that your Father who is in heaven will also forgive you your transgressions." The meaning is clear: you will not be heard by the Father if you do not forgive those who have hurt you.

Think about it. The whole essence of God's demonstrated Love toward us was and is that He forgave and forgives the sins of all those who have accepted His Son, Jesus Christ, as Savior and Lord. That is the model we, who are His, are to follow exactly. And if we won't or don't, then He is under no obligation to hear or answer our prayers (or for that matter to forgive our sins; see Mat 6:14,15 and Mk 11:26).

So, it is imperative that we keep short accounts with God and forgive all those we have something against, so He will hear and answer our prayers.

Praying and the Will of God

The first letter of John, in chapter 5, verse 14 makes it quite clear that we must pray in the will of God: "This is the confidence which we have before Him, that, if we ask anything according to His will, He hears us." So, then, how do we come to know His will? And can we know His will?

Yes, we can – if we are content to be fully surrendered to Him...to be held captive by Him. **We can know His will by asking Him to do His will**. Many of us are unwilling to pray that way; we want to know His will before we ask for Him to do His will. God probably does not disclose Himself to anyone who holds that kind of an attitude. Only the Christian whose will is surrendered to God can know His will. One of the purposes of prayer is to discover God's will in order that we might do it.

The more we get to know God personally through the study of His Word and prayerful meditation, the better we shall be able to know His will. Many of us fail right here. We must learn to discipline ourselves (what it means to be a disciple) to read and study the Bible prayerfully every day and to spend time in His presence. If you are not doing that faithfully and **with expectation**, you will be confused about God's will and your prayer life will be a failure.

I know that God has "spoken" to me both when I am reading His Word and when I am praying. But I am confident that when I do not spend time with Him in His Word and in prayer daily, I am like a sea captain lost at sea without a compass or a navigation chart.

Think of it this way. When you are with a good friend of many years, you often know what they are about to say. Why? Because by spending time with him or her over many years you have learned how they think. It's no different with God, our King of Kings – after years of our spending regular time with Him in His Word and in prayer, we know how He thinks about many things – so you begin to know His will for you.

Only the Christian whose will is surrendered to God can know His will.

Praying and Thanksgiving

It does not make sense to pray when I am not thankful to God for Who He is and what He has done in my life. Those who are ungrateful cannot expect to receive anything from God.

God wants us to pray and make requests of Him, but He expects us to come with a grateful spirit. The devil does not want us to pray, but if we feel we must, he is satisfied if we go through the motions of praying, as long as we remain unthankful. No sin is too small to hinder prayer and turn praying itself into sin. Praise is essential to prayer; look at Psalm 100:4 "Enter His gates with Thanksgiving, and His courts with Praise. Give thanks to Him, bless His name."

I have found that the more we reflect on God's goodness to us, the greater our "power" in prayer. It is a solemn duty to consider the rich blessings and benefits we have received from Him. If God never did another thing for any of us beyond Christ's Salvation, we would still owe Him our continual offering of thanks and praise forever!

And He has given us one of His most excellent commands with a promise in Philippians 4:6,7, "Be anxious for nothing, but in everything by prayer and supplication, **with thanksgiving**, let your requests be made known to God. And the Peace of God which surpasses all comprehension, will guard your hearts and minds in Christ Jesus." Again, note that we are to ask in thanksgiving. And who among us does not want His Peace, and who among us does not want His personal protection, His guardianship of our hearts and minds?

Praying and Abiding

If praying is a mystery to you, it might be that here is the key that will unlock the door to a full and joyful life.

"If you abide in Me, and My words abide in you, ask whatever you wish, and it will be done for you" (John 15:7, NASB). Ah, but bask with me in the incredible meaning of John 14:21..."He who has My commandments and keeps them is the one who loves Me; and he who loves Me will be loved by My Father, and I will love him and will disclose Myself to him."(NASB) This is truly why we pray – to have a close and ever deepening relationship with our almighty God!

So if you do not receive what you ask God for – it must be that He doesn't keep His promises – or – maybe, just maybe, we haven't met the condition. Which of those two do you think is the truth?

What does "abide" (Greek, *Meno*) mean? It means *to remain, continue, dwell, stay put.* If you are saved, then you do abide in Him (see Ephesians 5:30).

But the other condition concerns His Word abiding in us. And how is that accomplished? By regular – how about "daily" – prayer and reading and meditation on Scripture. We are branches grafted on to the Vine. We draw our nourishment from His "sap", His life-blood – which is through Communion in prayer and in taking in His Words in the Bible – by feeding on Him.

When we neglect the daily quiet, meditative reading of God's Word, we block the lifeline to God's throne of Grace.

Hear this, please. Our abiding in Christ and He in us through His Word is a life process that must never cease. When the Word of God is controlling our prayer life – "ask whatever you wish and it will be done for you."

And make no mistake, if it were not for God's Word, the Bible, I would not know how to pray or for what to pray.

But the mere reading of His Word in a mechanical fashion will not cause the Word to lodge in your heart. Read, then meditate, then obey. James said it bluntly in verse 22 of Chapter One of his letter: "But prove yourselves doers of the word and not merely hearers who delude themselves."

Finally, let me say that we do not pray to become spiritual, nor do we become spiritual by the saying of many prayers. When we pray the Bible way, it is because we are already spiritual. Only a spiritual Christian prays the way he ought to pray. And true spirituality can be arrived at only as God's Word is obeyed. The obedient Christian is the abiding Christian, and the abiding Christian enjoys an effective prayer life.

Praying and Giving

It does not make sense for a stingy Christian to ask anything of God. "He who shuts his ear to the cry of the poor, will also cry himself and not be answered." (Proverbs 21:13)

In that one verse of Scripture, you have a basic rule for successful praying. And yet, I will venture to guess that it is one of the least known of God's requirements to prevail in praying. It is not a new rule handed down recently by God, but an ancient one that has been bypassed for centuries by the majority of believers. And it is easy to see the reason why – it touches our money and earthly possessions. But there it is, like it or not.

God is the patron of the poor. He said, "One who is gracious to a poor man lends to the Lord, and He will repay him for his good deed." (Proverbs 19:17)

Those of us who are better provided for are expected to show compassion for the needy. God keeps records of our deeds, so we shall in no wise lose our reward if we share what we have with others. But woe be unto him who does not help a needy person who asks for it – especially a fellow Christian.

As an exercise, someday go through some of the Old Testament saints prayers. Prayers like Abraham's in Genesis 18 or Genesis 13 or Genesis 19. Abraham was mighty in prayer because he was generous in sharing with others.

Read Luke 6:38 to determine if God was as serious about this giving business affecting our well-being as it was in the Old. So, again, God is saying that He will be as generous with you as you are with others, no?

So the whole idea here is that we cannot expect to receive from God if we are unwilling to give. Once more, let's read 2 Corinthians 9:6-7; God looks favorably on those who give to help others in need, as it clearly states in the next verse (8). How about 1 John 3:22...

Some of us wrongly apply Philippians 4:19. Question: Is that for all of us or is there a condition that must first be met? What is that condition? (Hint: look at verse 18)

Though I am not advocating the incorrect understanding that we should give so we can get, there is truth to this whole issue that a generous giving to the Lord does guarantee a generous getting from the Lord, one that will meet all our material and spiritual needs. Just insure your heart is centered on the giving.

So, then, it just makes perfect sense to be a generous giver and helper of others, if we ever expect to receive from our God what we need. Let us all begin today to cultivate the Grace of Giving so that our prayers are not hindered.

Woe be unto him who does not help a needy person who asks for it – especially a fellow Christian.

Praying and the Marriage Relationship

It does not make sense for a husband or wife to make requests of God when the marriage relationship has broken down. As verses one and seven from Peter's first letter, chapter three, make quite clear, especially for husbands, the marriage relationship must be balanced as God wants it balanced, or praying will be hindered.

> *In the same way, you wives, be submissive to your own husbands so that even if any of them are disobedient to the word, they may be won without a word by the behavior of their wives... You husbands in the same way, live with your wives in an understanding way, as with someone weaker, since she is a woman; and show her honor as a fellow heir of the grace of life,* ***so that your prayers will not be hindered.*** (1 Peter 3:1,7)

The apostle Peter gets to the heart of this matter of prayer as it is affected by the husband-wife relationship. He warns all married couples that they had better shape up or suffer the hindrance of their own prayers.

For wives, it means that if you will not submit to your husband in all things then you are refusing to submit to the Lord, and such disobedience will hinder your prayer.

For husbands, when you fail to love your wife as Christ loves you and all others in His church, you cut off the power in praying and threaten your marriage.

Though there is much more that could be said here, we must remember that God makes the rules; our sole job is to Trust and Obey. And in the matter of love for one another, couples would do well to ponder verses 4 through 8 of 1 Corinthians 13, the great Love Chapter of the Bible.

Is there an antidote to these "hindrances" to effective praying? Of course. It is to confess, repent and to ask forgiveness for allowing one or more of these "hindrances" into your life. (1 John 1:9).

Praying and Fasting

It does not make sense to ignore the spiritual exercise of fasting as an aid to praying. Praying and fasting are linked together in several New Testament passages: Matthew 17:21; Mark 9:29; Luke 2:37; Acts 13:2,3; 14:23) The verb "to fast" (Greek, *nesteuo*) means *to abstain from eating*.

In prayer we draw near to God; in fasting we detach ourselves from something that could keep us from praying. When we fast, we must guard against a corrupt motive. God detests hypocrisy. Do your fasting in secret and live normally before your fellowmen.

If you need definitive information on Fasting and Prayer, I suggest you contact CRU.org and ask for their Fasting Starter Kit. It is an important resource for anyone being called to fast and pray.

Chapter Seven
Group Praying Habits to Avoid

Prominent praying is a show-off way of praying. It's done by persons who want to be seen by others as godly. The prayer itself may be genuine and needed, but if done for the motive of being seen as holy – it is a zero on God's chart.

> *When you pray, you are not to be like the hypocrites; for they love to stand and pray in the synagogues and on the street corners* ***so that they may be seen by men****. Truly I say to you, they have their reward in full.* (Matthew 6:5)

Pretense in praying suggests the show of something so as to disguise one's real self or motives. The word *pretense* is the translation of *prophasis*, meaning cloak. It suggests the show of something so as to disguise one's real self or motives. This is the terrible act of going through the motions of praying in an attempt to cover up some sin. Such a prayer is merely a pretense, or cloak, to conceal the real man.

Prolonged praying. Jesus spoke about those persons who make "long prayer." There are people who attach great importance to long prayers, thereby leading others to believe that the more saintly Christians spend much of their time on their knees, praying. **Don't fall into the lure of prolonged praying**. In Personal praying, pray a topic or two and then pause to hear from God. In group praying, pray only about one topic at a time and with one or two sentences, if possible; usually the group leader will specify the topic, but if not, curb your tendency to pray for everything on your heart. Give others a chance to pray, rather than "hog" the time with your concerns. It's just the simple courtesy of being considerate of others in your group; each person present deserves an opportunity to pray.

> *In His teaching, He was saying, 'Beware of the scribes who like to walk around in long robes, and ...who devour widows' houses, and for appearance's sake **offer long prayers**, these will receive greater condemnation.'* (Mark 12:38-40)

Preaching praying. This habit is too often experienced in the group or public prayer setting. I include it because most of us spend some time in group prayer settings and therefore we must know this habit and avoid it. Though I am unable to find a scripture reference to support a prohibition against this sort of praying, it is a close cousin to prolonged praying and pretense praying. I believe you will agree that it is a rude, even disrespectful, way to pray. It is rude and disrespectful to God, and it is rude to those who are present. If your group will pray as outlined for Conversational Prayer (Enclosure 4), you will more easily avoid this error.

Preaching praying occurs when someone is praying to God and then shifts gears, sometimes unwittingly, and begins to talk to the others in the group about some Scriptural or other issue, while still praying, ostensibly, with God.

That is like having a conversation with someone and then abruptly turning to and talking with one or more other people without excusing yourself from the first person to whom you were talking. Would you not agree that it is just plain rude, even disrespectful, especially as it pertains to praying with God? **Keep in mind to Whom you are talking – it is God Himself – so stay focused on Him.**

Secondly, God does not need your "lecture" on the meaning of some point of Scripture; after all, He wrote it and knows all about what it means. Not following this stricture also suggests you may unwittingly be seen by the group to hold yourself in some sort of superior position concerning Biblical knowledge – in that you feel you must lecture the others about some point of

Scripture which most of them are also familiar with and do not need your "lecture" any more than God does.

Now then, if you believe you have some point of instruction or insight you want to impart to the others in your prayer group, then close the praying respectfully and address your point to the group. Following that, you are free to return to praying.

So, again, **we must simply keep our minds tuned to Whom we are talking and that should be enough to curb the all-too-common practice of preaching or lecturing those with whom you are praying.** Think about it...

Finally, there is nothing wrong with and everything right with praying Scripture back to God as the Holy Spirit leads you to pray it. Frankly, using God's own Word to pray to Him in Praise or in petition probably pleases Him immensely. I pray some of the magnificent Praise Psalms to God as an uplifting way to give Him the praise He so richly deserves.

What we are talking about in Preaching Praying, however, is about lecturing God or those you are praying with about some aspect of Scripture. That is not prayer! If you need to preach, then preach. If you need to teach, then teach. But do not bury either one in prayer.

Chapter Eight
Thinking Through Your Praying Life

The best thing for you to do first – is to define what praying is to you, for you.

Is it conversation? Is it fellowship? Is it listening?
Is it being still before Him?
Is it enjoying our Great God as He wants us to enjoy Him, and He us?

Is it all of these from time to time?

Let me give you some work to do here. Look up and mark these scripture references in your own Bible to get the full effect...Jeremiah 29:11-13; Matthew 6:5-15; Ephesians 2:18; 6:18. Then read through these references for a bit more depth.

Adam, before falling, walked and talked with God in close fellowship. (Genesis 1:27-30)

Calling upon the name of the Lord (First done in Genesis 4:26 by Enosh)

Enoch lived in close fellowship with God, then God took him up. (Genesis 5:24)

He hears us... (Psalms 34:15; 18:6; 1 Peter 3:12; Psalm 66:19,20)

He answers us... (Acts 9:40; 1 Samuel 1:10-17; 2 Kings 20:1-6)

"The Lord is near to all who call upon Him, to all who call upon Him in Truth." (Psalm 145:18)

"Seek the Lord while He may be found, call upon Him while He is near." (Isaiah 55:6)

"...with all who in every place call upon the name of our Lord Jesus Christ..." (1 Corinthians 1:2)

"I love the Lord because He hears my voice and my supplication. Because He has inclined His ear to me, therefore I shall call on Him as long as I live." (Psalm 116:1,2)

"Don't worry about anything; instead, pray about everything. Tell God what you need, and thank Him for all He has done." (Philippians 4:6)

Let this be your heart's desire:
"Lord, make this clay house, my body,
a House of Purity, Prayer, and Praise for Your glory!"

Scripture Suggests Several Plans for Praying!
Is a plan helpful...or necessary? Are we looking for a formula?

Plan One

2 Chronicles 7:14 - Humble yourself, pray, seek My face, turn from your wicked ways (then God will hear, forgive, and heal the land)

Humble yourself – ask forgiveness, cleansing, acknowledge His Holiness. (Psalm 24:3,4)

Pray – come into His presence rejoicing with supplications.

Seek His Face – ask Him what He wants you to do; look Him straight in the eye – face to face, as it were. Same as when your boss tasks you with a job to do.

Turn from your wicked ways – so that we remain pure, a light to others, an example to others about Him. (Psalm 139:23,24)

Plan Two

Dr. Strauss questions if our Lord's objective in the so-called (and misnamed) "Lord's Prayer" was to provide a prayer to be recited by His followers. Dr. Strauss believed that Jesus was giving us a formulary, or model, of how to pray and for what to pray.

Dr. Larry Lea, while pastor of the mega-church, Church on the Rock, in Rockwall, Texas in the late 1980's wrestled with God about how to better pray. Over time, God told him how to use the Lord's Prayer as an outline for detailed and thorough prayer.

So on the strength of two God-given insights as well as my own experience, I will have to say that we have in this marvelous prayer, a pattern for praying.

The Disciple's Prayer. (Matthew 6:9-12, and Luke 11:2-4; see Enclosure 5)

Also known as the "Lord's Prayer", it is both a prayer and an outline for an even richer time when alone with our Lord. As you discipline yourself to come regularly into God's presence, using this God-given "tool", praying will become your life flow, your spiritual breathing, as it was for Jesus.

Consider that Jesus, the Son of God, spent a fourth or more of His ministry life in solitary prayer with His Father God. If He, being God and perfect man, could spend that amount of time with His Father, how much then should we, as saved sinners and imperfect humans, be "willing" to spend in conversation and meditation with Him?!

Remember – the power of God comes to each of our lives as well as to the church on the wings of prayer! And through our solitary times of concentrated prayer with our God, we can also develop a sense of actually being in the Presence of God throughout each day – as did Jesus, as He walked and prayed and did His Father's will.

If you do not begin to pray, you will not be any further along with the Lord next year than you are right now. The Spirit of God wants to teach you to walk in the yoke He has fitted for you. And His yoke is easy and His burden light (Mat 11:30). He invites you to spend time with Him in that yoke – which means He is taking at least half your load.

Every devoted Christ-follower wants to become more like our Savior. But change demands the discipline of persistence. We must be determined in our pursuit of God – determined to wait upon Him, letting Him tell us what His will is. Then the change we seek begins to rise in us like the sun coming up in the morning.

God is also looking for believers who will stand in the gap and intercede on behalf of others. He invites our worship of Him, for our sakes, not His. He longs for servants who will tarry in His presence until they are endowed with power from on high to then go out to do His bidding. In short, God wants us to walk with Him and talk with Him. Remember Enoch in Genesis 5:22,24: "He walked with God; and he was not, for God took him." How greatly pleased with Enoch's devotion to Him He was – so He just brought him home a bit early (he was only 365 years young).

Let this be your heart's desire: "Lord, make this clay house, my body, a House of Purity, Prayer, and Praise for Your glory!"

The Disciple's Prayer at Enclosure 5 (developed by God through Pastor Larry Lea) is for your personal use in your private prayer each morning. We suggest going over it section by section. If you decide to use this as your outline for prayer, you can tuck a copy of it in your Bible. Share this idea and give copies away, teach others...

Plan Three

CATSS - Confession, Adoration, Thanksgiving, Supplication, Song, Enclosure 3

Confession – Cleansing self first – why? Psalm 66:18 makes it clear that unconfessed sin assures that God will not hear my prayer, and Psalm 24:3,4 suggests that only those who have clean hands and a pure heart, may ascend up to the hill of (climb the mountain to) the Lord. So it seems best to cleanse ourselves of all unrighteousness by confession and repentance before the Lord prior to embarking on any other aspect of our praying (1 John 1:9).

Though not for the same purpose (He needed no forgiveness), even Jesus in His marvelous High Priestly Prayer in John 17, begins by bringing Himself before the Lord – and then goes on to pray for others. An example worthy of emulation...

Adoration – Come into His gates with thanksgiving and into His courts with praise (Psalm 100:4,5).

This next accumulation of scriptures will give you an excellent time of worship and adoration as you go through each one. Some may become your favorite worship verses. So, offer Him unrestrained praise and worship. (Exodus 15:1-18; 1 Samuel 2:1-10; 1 Chronicles 16:28,29; 29:10-19; Psalms 8; 9; 18; 19; 22:3; 24; 30; 50:23; 65; 92; 104; 108; 138; 139; 147-150; Luke 1:46-55; 19:37,38; Ephesians 3:20,21; 5:18,19; 1 Timothy 1:17; Hebrews 13:21; 1 Peter 2:5; Jude 25; Revelation 5:9-14; 7:9-17; 15:3,4; 19:1-7 and others)

Thanksgiving – Offer Him thanks for **all** He has done for you and yours.

Supplication

Ask Him to tell you what He wants you to pray about.

Ask Him for appropriate specific help for others He has brought to your mind – especially those needing Jesus.

Ask Him for your needs, for blessings, for protection...

Ask for His blessings & directions for our authorities, saved or not. (Romans 13:7)
Ask Him to give you His heart for the lost (then, look out!).
Ask Him to bless and protect your spouse, your family, your church leaders and their families, especially your Pastor and Elders and their families.
Ask Him to give you help to forgive those who have hurt you.

Song – Sing His Praises again – for He alone is worthy of our Praise...

What we have just covered here is the front part of what can be a much broader prayer time. The Prayer Guide (Enclosure 3) uses this Plan Three up front but then goes on to much more. It can become a complete prayer outline for covering many more of the possible topics that need to be lifted up to God.

Another prayer resource is a copy of your church's directory; praying for one page of names of the people in your church per week. Still another is to pray over the news topics you have heard about or read about.

Lastly, I have included a section on The Prayer Life of Jesus (Enclosure 6). Let's just simply all agree that the greatest Teacher and Pray-or Who ever lived can still teach us about a lot of things – especially praying. I commend to you a close reading of it.

Chapter Nine
Concluding Thoughts

Spending more time talking with our loving God and even **listening** more than speaking, will inevitably conform us more into His likeness. And there is no higher goal for a blood-bought, sold-out child of God than to become more like our Heavenly Father...more like Jesus, our Christ...

The day always seems to go better when we have started it with Him.

You can achieve this by the simple, but often difficult expedient of:

1) getting out of bed 40-60 minutes earlier,
2) going to your "quiet place",
3) reading a chapter or so of His Word (using a study bible is an excellent reading help, or using a daily devotional like Moody's "Today in the Word" is helpful for some), and then,
4) talking with God about what is on your mind and ***what is on His mind for you.*** Most of us who have determined to follow this regimen, even though dead-tired on some mornings, leave our Quiet Time with God much refreshed and truly energized for the day's demands. The day always seems to go better when we have started it with Him. "Do not be afraid or discouraged. For the Lord your God is with you wherever you go." (Joshua 1:9). Though promised to Joshua, it surely applies to all of us who seek after God and His will for us.

And that is another valuable facet of this jewel called Praying. Because He is with us as we journey through each day, as we encounter barriers, hindrances, roadblocks and delays, we can turn to Him instantly in our minds and hearts and ask Him for advice and help. We may (and should) want to praise and thank Him throughout the day when He has made our rough places smooth, our difficulties disappear, and our burdens lighter. You may even want to regularly use a prayer journal to record your petitions and His answers; many do so. Then, on those days when you are "down", you can reread portions of your prayer journal and be blessed all over again by His previous blessings!

So, praying is our great privilege to speak with our Maker about all manner of issues, and more importantly, to hear from Him! Obviously it opens the path to greater learning about Him from Him. Perhaps you would agree that it is a privilege that we can ill afford to neglect. After all, why wouldn't we truly want to become conformed to the very image of our God? He originally created us to that end – to become His image exactly. Then sin entered in, mankind and all of creation became corrupted. Yet, through repentance and Christ's agonizingly shed blood, we who believe are redeemed – saved *from* hell and <u>for</u> heaven – and our eternal life in Him begins exactly at that moment of our heavenly salvation! Soli Deo Gloria!

So why wouldn't we want to change our priorities and begin to spend much more time with Him? He wants you to do it – **for your own good.** Do you?

A short booklet that you may find delightfully convicting is: "My Heart – Christ's Home" by Robert Boyd Munger, ISBN 978-0-87784-075-6

* *

Lastly, let me share with you a powerful but beautiful devotional written by Worship Pastor Keith Ferguson of First Baptist Church at the Fields, Carrollton, Texas.

Lord, Hear My Prayer

O Lord, hear me as I pray; pay attention to my groaning. Listen to my cry for help, my King and my God, for I pray to no one but you. Listen to my voice in the morning, Lord. Each morning I bring my requests to you and wait expectantly. Psalm 5:1-3

When we read the psalms – most of them written by King David – we read honest and transparent moments of emotion. Moments of anger, depression, sorrow, fear . . . negative thoughts that Christians are often taught to never express, or worse – suppress.

King David is wise enough to know that he should not suppress these thoughts but take them to the only place where he can find help and healing. He takes them directly to God in prayer. In just three verses from Psalm 5, we see hope in the midst of discouragement. He pleads with God to hear his cry for help and then declares by faith that the Lord hears his voice and David determines to wait expectantly for Him to answer.

Note how simple this prayer is. You cannot escape that David pursues a personal, intimate relationship with God and feels free to call out to Him in a direct and personal way. This enables David to seek peace from the only One capable to bring peace.

Irish poet Joseph Scriven (1819-1886) struggled with depression. His first fiancé drowned the night before their wedding. Falling in love again, his second fiancé died of pneumonia. In 1855, as his mother lay dying, Scriven wrote a poem – "Pray Without Ceasing".

What a friend we have in Jesus, all our sins and griefs to bear.
What a privilege to carry everything to God in prayer.
Oh, what peace we often forfeit, oh, what needless pain we bear.
All because we do not carry everything to God in prayer.
Have we trials and temptations? Is there trouble anywhere?
We should never be discouraged, take it to the Lord in prayer.
Can we find a friend so faithful who will all our sorrows share?
Jesus knows our every weakness, take it to the Lord in prayer.

1. Has God ever delivered you from discouragement through prayer? Thank Him.

2. Are you suppressing negative emotions that you should "take to the Lord in prayer"?

And his closing prayer that each of us can and should pray:

Lord Jesus, You beckon me – "Come to Me,
all who are weak and heavy
laden, and I will give you rest." Forgive me
for turning to anyone
or anything with my burdens before I first
come to You in prayer.
You alone can meet my need! Amen...

* *

Praying is our great privilege to speak with our Maker about all manner of issues, and more importantly, to hear from Him!

Hope is found in only one place – in the wise and faithful rule of your Father in heaven. Prayer is never about asking God to submit His awesome power to your will and plan; prayer is an act of personal submission to the always-right will of God. When you're joyfully willing to submit to the will of this One, you know grace has taken residence in your heart. Paul David Tripp from his book *New Morning Mercies*, May 7.

When God is about to do a work on the earth, He always starts by waking up His people and calling them back to prayer.

Epilogue

This short treatise is an intended teaching resource about Praying. I also recommend the excellent six-week training course entitled "Pray in Faith" by T.W. Hunt and Claude King. It's a Lifeway Press book and part of the Growing Disciple Series.

As was said earlier, "the power of God comes to a person, a people, or a church on the wings of praying." There is no better place for all God's people to agree in praying than in God's House – the House of Prayer. **Praying in the church during each Worship Service, on a designated church wide prayer night, during every Bible Study, and wherever else His Holy Spirit leads us to pray appears to be what God has in mind.** Think about it! Pray about it! Perhaps you can be a catalyst to start Group Praying in your church – or join in on what God is already doing in your church about Praying.

A word about Bible Translations. There are two translation methods. One is Literal, the other is Dynamic Equivalence. English translations of the Bible are much improved from the archaic English syntax of the 15th and 16th centuries as wonderful as was the King James Version when it first appeared. As more was learned about the ancient written Greek and Hebrew languages, clarity of intended meanings resulted. **Knowing what the Bible says and means is critical to personal understanding and growth.** Quite simply I must recommend you use a modern version of the Bible in the Study Bible format. The Life Application Study Bible is among the very best of these.

One of the finest recent (2004) easy-reading, dynamic-equivalence translations is the New Living Translation from Tyndale House Publishers. Another excellent translation is the New American Standard Bible, updated in 1997 and published by The Lockman Foundation. Each of these is available as a Life Application Study Bible. **Always use a thoroughly accurate**

and easily understood translation of the Holy Bible to help you grow wise in His ways.

One of the truly marvelous modern advantages for Bible Study or Reading is that we are able to store one or more translations of the Bible on our Smartphones. We are even able to store a full Life Application Study Bible in one or more of the translations. In effect, we are able to carry around with us at all times a readily available and useful Study Bible library, and not be encumbered by carrying a large, heavy book or books.

Principal References

The New American Standard Bible ®, Copyright © 1960,1962, 1963, 1968, 1971, 1972, 1973, 1975, 1977, 1995 by The Lockman Foundation. Used by permission.

Holy Bible, New Living Translation, copyright © 1996, 2004. Used by permission of Tyndale House Publishers, Inc., Wheaten, Illinois 60189. All rights reserved.

Strauss, Lehman. "Sense and Nonsense About Prayer", The Moody Bible Institute of Chicago, 1974 (eleventh printing 1981). ISBN 0-8024-7702-X

<u>Enclosures</u>

1. Additional Reading
2. Intercessory Praying
3. A Guide for Praying
4. Conversational Praying
5. The Disciple's Prayer
6. Jesus' Praying Life
7. Praying: Selected Scriptures
8. Praying Evidences in the Bible

Enclosure One – Additional Reading

Barton, David	America: To Pray or Not to Pray?
Bennett, Dennis J.	Nine O'clock in the Morning
Boice, James Montgomery	Awakening to God
Bounds, E.M.	The Complete Works of E.M. Bounds on Prayer
Brueggeman, Walter	Praying the Psalms
Cho, Paul Yonggi	The Fourth Dimension
Cornwall, Judson	Praying the Scriptures
Cymbala, Jim	Fresh Wind, Fresh Fire
Dawson, Joy	Intimate Friendship with God
Duewel, Wesley L.	Ablaze for God
Duewel, Wesley L.	Mighty Prevailing Prayer
Elliff, Tom	A Passion for Prayer Experience Deeper Intimacy with God
Finney, Charles G.	Principles of Prayer
Goll, Jim W.	The Lost Art of Intercession
Gordon, S.D.	Quiet Talks on Prayer
Grubb, Norman	Rees Howells, Intercessor
Gruen, Ernest	Touching the Heart of God
Hallesby, O.	Prayer
Hayford, Jack	Prayer is Invading the Impossible
Hunt, T.W.	The Doctrine of Prayer
Hunt and Walker	Pray in Faith

Knowles, Andrew	Discovering Prayer
LeSourd, Leonard E.	Touching the Heart of God
Munroe, Myles	Understanding the Purpose and Power of Prayer
Murray, Andrew	With Christ in the School of Prayer
Nander Griend, Alvin J. w/ Edith Bajema	The Praying Church Sourcebook, 2nd Ed. CRC Pubs, Grand Rapids, MI, 1997
Osteen, John	How to Release the Power of God
Packer, J .I .	Knowing God
Price, Oliver W.	The Power of Praying Together
Raybon, Patricia	I Told the Mountain to Move
Rice, John R.	Prayer – Asking and Receiving
Slosser, Bob	Miracle In Darien
Smith, Chuck	Effective Prayer Life
Spurgeon, Charles H.	Spurgeon on Prayer - How to Converse with God
Thrasher, Bill	A Journey to Victorious Praying
Tims, David	Living the Lord's Prayer
Torrey, R.A.	The Power of Prayer
Towns, Elmer L.	Praying the Lord's Prayer-for Spiritual Breakthrough
Tozer, A.W.	The Pursuit of God
Various Authors	Prayer – Its Deeper Dimensions
Wagner, C. Peter	Churches That Pray

Walker, Catherine & T.W. Hunt	Disciple's Prayer Life
Willhite, B.J.	Why Pray?
Yancey, Philip	Prayer: Does It Make Any Difference?
Yonggi Cho, Paul	The Fourth Dimension

<u>Workbook for a Course on Prayer</u>

Hunt, T.W. & Catherine Walker	Disciples Prayer Life – Walking in Fellowship with God

Enclosure Two – Intercessory Praying

NOTES FOR INTERCESSORS

Author: Unknown

Intercession, Greek – Huperentongehano...may be defined as "a more exceedingly excellent conferring with the Almighty, principally on behalf of others." It is more exceedingly excellent because it is not mere prayer initiated by man, but man praying out God–initiated prayers and empowered by the Spirit.

An intercessor must first of all be a believer – "He that comes to God must believe that He is". Heb 11:6 (Jn 14:1) "No one comes to the Father, but by me." Jn 14:6 (Jn 9:31, 3:3-18, Ac 4:12) "For through Jesus Christ we have access to the Father by the Holy Spirit." Ep 2:18. (1Co 2:10-14) "Everyone who calls on the name of the Lord shall be saved." Ro 10-13

Know the Lord, for without the Lord you can do nothing (Jn 15:5) Cultivate an intimate relationship with the Lord. Take time with Him talking, praising, listening..."hear" Him. "If ye abide in me and my words abide in you, you shall ask what you will, and it shall be done unto you.' Jn 15:7 (Jn 10:27, Lk 10:39, Mt 16:15-17, Ph 3:10, 1 Jn 5:15, 20)

Know the Word...study, memorize, meditate on. "Thy word is a lamp unto my feet, and a light unto my path." Ps 119:105 God's direction is always consistent with His word, character and ways as revealed in Scripture. (2Ti 2:15, 3:16)

Ask for the Fear of the Lord, a reverence for God, an understanding of His holiness, and a hatred of evil the way God hates it. Ask God to restore your conscience where sin or unforgiveness have seared and made it dull to righteousness and the convicting power of the Holy Spirit. (Ps 33:8, 25:14, Pr 2:5, 8:13, 9:10, 13:5, 14:26, 2 Ch 19:7, 9, Heb 12:28)

Ask for the Love of God that casts out all (ungodly) fear, enabling us to love Him with our whole heart, drawing us to an intimate relationship with Himself, compelling us to keep His commands, obey His word, and devotedly serve Him. "The love of God is shed abroad in our hearts by the Spirit." Ro 5:5 (Ro 8:35-39, 1 Jn 4:16, Jn 13:35, Mt 22:37, 2 Jn 6, Ja 1:12, 2-5)

Ask God for discernment; to discern what you "hear," and wisdom to rightly handle the word, knowledge and understanding He gives. (1Co 12:8,10, 2:14, Ja 1:5, Heb 5:14, 1 Jn 4:1, 1K 3:9-12, Eze 44:23, Pr 2:6, 4:7)

God may call you to fast and pray. You may choose to fast and pray, or you may find that your time in prayer before the Lord has resulted in a fast. Sometimes a break-through or victory sought can only be gained when fasting is coupled with prayer. (Da 10:3, Ex 34:28, Es 4:16, Joel 1:14, Is 58:6-12, Mt 17:21, 4:1-2,6:16-18, Jona 3:5)

Prayer power increases with united prayer, as two or more "agree in prayer," and as we pray in "one accord" (Mt 18:18-20, Ac 1:14,4:24, Le 26:8, Is 30:17, Ec 4:12) *Group note: Keep intercession groups small. If the number of intercessors present exceeds six or seven, break up into two groups. It is easier for most of us to speak up or pray out loud if the group is small. Exception: when God calls us to life up our voices in prayer or praise together…in one accord.

Intercession is not a sign of spirituality. Take prayer seriously, but don't take yourself too seriously. Pride has to prove itself or make things happen. It is God who confirms His word with signs following, in His way and time. (Mk 16:20) Be teachable, in right relationship with God and man, and let all things be done to edify. (1Co 14:26, Ga 5:14) "So you also, when you have done everything you were told to do, should say, "We are unworthy servants, we have only done our duty." Lk 17:10. (Jn. 13:16, Is 42:8, Ep 4:2-32, 5:21, 2 Ch 7:14)

Unless God prompts you to share, remain silent! Be discreet, be wise in sharing any of what God has revealed in intercession. "Mary kept all these things and pondered them in her heart." Lk 2:19 "And they kept silent and told no one in those days anything of what they had seen." Lk 9:36 (Ps 25:14, 19:18, Pr 2:10,3:21,5:2,11:13,17:28,20:19,Is 28:26)

Intercession may include "spiritual warfare." At times the battle in the spiritual realm must first be won before the victory can be established in the natural realm. Standing "in Christ" (the armor of God) upon the finished work of Calvary, from the believer's position with Christ seated in the heavenlies, with the authority given the believer...wield the mighty "weapons of our warfare" (the Name of Jesus Christ, the power of His Blood, the Word (God's Word [Sword of the Spirit] and the word of our testimony), in specific, Spirit-directed, Spirit-empowered, persistent prayer, extending the victory Jesus has already gained over Satan by His death and resurrection. Goal: win the war and possess the land by living an honest, upright life; walking in the Spirit, in repentance, forgiveness, obedience, love, truth mercy and grace; moving in the opposite spirit of the devil. (Ps 149, Ep 2:6,6:12, Ro13:14,Lk10:19, 2Co 10:3,4 Mt 4:10,12:29,18:18, Da 10:13,20, Zec 4:6)

Binding and loosing. "Assuredly, I say to You, whatever you bind on earth shall be (has been, is being) bound in heaven, and whatever you loose on earth shall be (has been, is being) loosed in heaven." Mt 18:18. There are times the strong man (demonic spirit) must be bound in the power and authority of the Name and Blood of Jesus, before prayers are effectual. "How can one enter into a strong man's house, and spoil his goods, unless he first "bind" the strongman? Then he will spoil his house." Mt 12:29.

Parameters of prayer. Pray within your God-given area of responsibility, authority, anointing (2Co 10:13). God, Jesus, the Holy Spirit, angels, the Church and the believer – each has his part in spiritual warfare. (Rev 12:7-11, 2 Ch 32:21, Zec 4:6, Mt 16:18, Jude 9, Zec 3:2, Lk 9:1, 2 Pe 2:11, Ac 19:13).

Important intercessors of the Bible: Abraham (Ge 18:23-33), Moses (Nu 14:11-20, Ex 32:32, De 9:25, Ps 106:23), Nehemiah (Ne 1:4-11), Ezra (Ezr 9:4-15), Daniel (Da 9:3-22), Paul (Ro 9:3,4:19), Col 1:9), and of course Jesus (Ro 8:34, 11:2, He 7:25, Is 53:12, Lk 22:31,24:34, Jn 17:9-26). Consider the contents of their prayers: fasting, humbling, weeping, persevering, identifying with the people, honest, appraisal, confession and repentance of specific personal, corporate, national, and ancestral sins (except Jesus); with continual reference to God's character, His Word, people, work, responsibility, promises, justice, mercy, and His glory. Others: Joshua, Job, Samuel, Elijah, David, Solomon, Isaiah, Stephen, prophets, priests, the people of God. (Is 62:6, Joel 2:15-18, Es 4:14-16, Je 7:16,9:17,11:14,14:11,15:1, 27:18, 2 Ch 7:14)

Avoid the temptation to become discouraged. Victory is found by those who prevail. Too often we quit too soon before the battle is truly won. Daniel prayed 21 days until he received the answer from God. Anna prayed at least 60 years for the coming of the Messiah before she beheld the answer. (Da 10:3,12,13, Lk 2:36-38,18:1, Heb 6:12-15, 2Sa 12:22,23)

God answers prayer, having considered all the implications from His perspective, in the light of eternity.

BE ENCOURAGED * BE PERSISTENT * BE PATIENT * BE FAITHFUL TO PRAY

PRAYER IS NEVER WASTED!

Enclosure Three – A Guide for Praying

Yourself – C.A.T.S.S. – Confession, Adoration, Thanksgiving, Supplication, Song… Confession precedes worship because He must be worshipped and served by a humbled heart, and a vessel made clean and holy by His forgiveness through our repentance. See Ps 24:3,4; 66:18; and 1 Jn 1:9. Therefore it's prudent to square ourselves away with the Lord first, before we tackle other burdens He has placed on our hearts. Jesus, though perfect, did just this as a model for us in His High Priestly Prayer (Jn 17). Pray always for your own **personal revival**!

Our God
That He will be Glorified and blessed by all we think, say or do – so that others may see Him in us & ask us about the "hope" that is in us (1 Pet 3:15).

Our Own Family, our extended family's members…& our friends…
Salvation for all, healing for the afflicted, restoration of relationships…

His Church
Revival! (2 Chron 7:13,14… note that "humble themselves" is God's first requirement of us. See also Isaiah 6:1-6.) That He will call all His Shepherds to "Pray and Seek His Face"… That we all have courage to be Salt & Light (1 Cor 16:13,14), standing firmly on the Rock of Salvation! Always pray for His special people Israel – pray for the peace of Jerusalem…

"Our" Local Church
Again, pray for revival. Pray for God's guidance and protection - Pastor, Elders, Deacons, Leaders, Teachers, Staff, Missionaries, Youth, Students, Members, Attenders… That He will deal mercifully with those members afflicted and infirm…Will help us catch the vision & resolve to give more of ourselves & "our" treasure to serve the Body more faithfully, to share Christ

diligently with family, friends, workers, neighbors & merchants...to become more like Christ!

Our Missionaries
Pray for their protection, provision and great success in sharing the Gospel

Our National, State & Local Governments
Pray blessings, wisdom & salvation for our President & Governors, Cabinet Officials & Advisors, Congressmen & Legislators, Supreme Court Justices & Other Court Officers, all Judges. County Commissioners, Mayors, & all government staffers. Ask Him to once again give us godly men & women to lead us. That He will frustrate the intentions of those tending toward tyranny & instead ensure our liberty (Pr 21:1).

Our Nation's Businesses, Industry, Schools, Media, Entertainment...
That He will prosper those persons & organizations dedicated to following His will in all things... That He will dry up the funds & other resources of those organizations opposed to His will... That He will forgive our turning away from Him and bring us back to Himself in all these areas.

Our Armed Forces
Pray for wisdom, mercy & courageous hearts for our Civilian & Military Leaders, Soldiers, Sailors, Marines, Airmen, & others. Grant them salvation, protection and victory.

Our Enemies
Their Salvation. Their defeat by force or by denying them resources. (Ps 54:4,5; 140:9-11)

Enclosure Four – Conversational Praying

Group prayer was a characteristic of the early Christians. We read in Acts 12:12 that Peter went to the house of Mary where many were gathered for prayer. Earlier in Acts, we read that the disciples "went up to the upper room, where they were staying…. These all with one mind were continually devoting themselves to prayer, along with the women" (Acts 1:13–14). Old Testament characters also participated in group prayer. For example, 2 Chronicles 6:13–42 records Solomon praying as all Israel gathered around.

During a time of conversational prayer, the group members talk to God the same way they would talk to a friend who is in the room with them. Members should use everyday conversational language. Encourage the group (especially a group unfamiliar with group prayer) to feel free **to pray in one or two sentence prayers**, expressing only a brief thought in a few words. Please don't pray long, elaborate prayers. Be considerate of others; don't monopolize the conversation with God. Group praying is a dialogue, not a monologue.

Everyone is free to pray, or not to pray, as the Spirit directs. Don't be concerned about silence – allow God to speak to you and the other individuals in the group during times of silence. And as with normal conversation, there is no need to pray in order around the group, but pray as you would converse in a roomful of people – as the moment is right for you to speak.

Remember that the purpose of your prayer is to communicate with God. It should never be viewed as a ritual or as a time to "preach" to one another.

Ways to lead conversational prayer:

Several different ways of leading conversational prayer are discussed below. You could choose one of these methods to guide your prayer time or use several to provide variety.

Leader-introduced topics: Introduce a prayer topic or request, one at a time. The group will then pray about this topic or request. When finished, the leader will introduce another topic or request. Both the number and types of topics introduced may vary. It is always helpful to designate a specific person to close each time. This helps ensure that the prayer time will not bog down when everyone has had the opportunity to pray if they so desire.

Shared prayer requests: Allow the group to share prayer requests. As a prayer request is offered, you could ask another member to be responsible to pray for that request during the prayer time. This ensures that each person's request will be prayed for by at least one other person.

You might want to have group members record on a sheet of paper each request as it is given. They could then refer to the list during the group prayer time as well as throughout the week as a reminder to continue to pray for one another. You could allow group members to volunteer to pray for requests without assigning them or writing them down. The group would then rely on their memories during the prayer time.

You may wish to pray for each request as soon as it is given, before the next request is shared.

Pray through Scripture: This method allows the group to use one or more passages of scripture as a prayer guide. You can choose any passage that you feel will be appropriate. Here are some examples:

Choose a Psalm of praise, such as Psalm 103, Psalm 145 or Psalm 150.

Teach the group to pray using the following procedure:

1. The first person reads a phrase or an entire verse aloud, pausing to pray a simple prayer as inspired by the scripture and led by the Lord.

2. Other members of the group join in audibly or silently agree.

3. The next person reads a different verse, pausing to pray aloud as he is impressed by the Lord.

4. Continue the same way around the group.

Enclosure Five – The Disciple's Prayer

From Larry Lea's Book "Could You Not Tarry One Hour?"
Expanded from Matthew 6:9-13

I. "Our Father which art in heaven, Hallowed be thy name."

A. Picture Calvary and thank God you can call Him Father by virtue of the blood of Jesus.

B. Hallow the names of God corresponding with the five benefits in the New Covenant, and make your faith declarations.

Benefit	Name	Meaning
SIN	*JEHOVAH-TSIDKENU*	The Lord My Righteousness
	JEHOVAH-M'KADDESH	The Lord Who Sanctifies
SPIRIT	*JEHOVAH-SHALOM*	The Lord is Peace
	JEHOVAH-SHAMMAH	The Lord is There
SOUNDNESS	*JEHOVAH-ROPHE*	The Lord Who Heals
SUCCESS	*JEHOVAH-JIREH*	The Lord's Provision Shall Be Seen
SECURITY	*JEHOVAH-NISSI*	The Lord My Banner
	JEHOVAH – ROHI	The Lord My Shepherd

II. "Thy kingdom come. Thy will be done."

A. Yourself

B. Your family (mate, children, other family members)

C. Your church (pastor, leadership, faithfulness of the people, harvest)

D. Nation (city, state and national political and spiritual leaders, a specific nation)

III. "Give us this day our daily bread"
A. Be in the will of God (prayer life, church, work habits, obedience in giving).
B. Believe it is God's will to prosper you.
C. Be specific
D. Be tenacious

IV. "And forgive us our debts as we forgive our debtors"
A. Ask God to forgive you.
B. Forgive and release others.
C. Set your will to forgive those who sin against you.

V. "And lead us not into temptation, but deliver us from evil."
A. Put on the whole armor of God, the Lord Jesus Christ
1. Loins girt about with truth
2. Breastplate of righteousness
3. Feet shod with the preparation (readiness) of the gospel of peace
4. Shield of faith
5. Helmet of salvation
6. Sword of the Spirit, which is the word (rhema) of God

B. PRAY a hedge of protection. (The Lord is your refuge, your fortress, your God; in Him will you trust)
1. Because you have made the Lord your habitation
2. Because you have set your love upon Him
3. Because you have known His name

VI. "For thine is the kingdom, and the power, and the glory, for ever."
A. Make your faith declarations
B. Return to praise.

* *

Prayer is abandoning my addiction to other glories and delighting. in the one glory that is truly glorious – the Glory of God!

This is a special insight into the Lord's/Disciple's Prayer
from *New Morning Mercies*, April 2. a Daily Gospel Devotional
by Paul David Tripp

Sadly, prayer for many of us has been shrunk to an agenda that is little bigger than asking God for stuff. It has become that spiritual place where we ask God to sign our personal wish lists. For many, it is little more than a repeated cycle of requesting, followed by waiting to see if God, in fact, comes through. If he does, we celebrate his faithfulness and love; but if he doesn't, we not only wonder if he cares, we are also tempted to wonder if he's there. In this way, prayer often amounts to shopping at the Trinitarian department store for things that you have told yourself you need with the hope that they will be free.

But consider the Lord's Prayer for a moment. *It doesn't look anything like what I've just described. This prayer is a prayer of worship and surrender. It recognizes, at the deepest level, the war that still goes on in my heart between the kingdom of self and Kingdom of God. It faces the fact that I can be so blind to the glory of God, and as I am, I become captured by the small glories of the created world. It does more surrendering and celebrating than it does asking. And the asking that it does is in the context not of self-glory wishing, but rather in the context of submission and worship.*

How does this prayer begin? It begins by reminding you of the most astounding reality of your life. It begins with a celebration of grace: ***"Our Father in heaven…"*** *(Matt. 6:9a). You and I must never stop celebrating this reality. God, the Creator, King, Savior, and Lord exercised his power and grace so that people like us would become his children. What's next?* ***"Hallowed be your name"*** *(v. 9b). Here I surrender myself to the agenda of agendas. It is the reason the world was made. It is why you and I were created. It was all brought into being so that God would get the glory that He is due. Here I let go of all the other glories that may lay claim to my wandering heart. Here I find my motivation for all that I do. Here I cry out for rescuing grace for my disloyal heart.*

Then this model prayer hits its bottom line. The next words contain a comfort and a call: ***"Your kingdom come, your will be done, on earth as it is in heaven"*** *(v.10) The comfort is that the Father, in redeeming love, has graciously chosen to give* *us his kingdom. He blesses us with his rule, which is always wise loving, faithful, true, gracious, and good, and in so doing, rescues us from our little kingdoms of one. The call is to let go of our Vise-Grip hold on our Lilliputian kingdoms and give ourselves to his kingdom of glory and grace. It is only when our hearts have been protected by the worship and celebration of these requests that we are able to properly pray what comes next.*

Enclosure Six – Jesus' Praying Life

(Selected Quotes from Lehman Strauss' Book "*Sense and Nonsense about Prayer,*" Chapter 15)

Our Lord Jesus Christ instructed His disciples to pray, and in so doing He taught them by precept. But the greater impact was made upon their lives when they watched and heard Him pray. His prayer life was an illustration of how they should pray, teaching them by His example. We preach, and then we struggle to practice that which we have preached, but Jesus preached what He practiced. He taught much about prayer, but He also loved to pray. Praying was a natural part of His life: to Him it was like breathing.

Let us spend a few minutes in the school of prayer and learn how Jesus prayed. It is important that we study what He said about prayer, but it is equally important that we know how and when He prayed. He was surrounded by the same circumstances, which touch our lives, and prayer was the mighty weapon, which He used repeatedly.

In the four gospel records, there are not less than fifteen recorded occasions on which Christ prayed. From these we may learn lessons that can strengthen us in our own prayer life. We will not examine all fifteen passages in their chronological order, but rather we will attempt to present a composite picture and glean lessons from the whole.

HIS MINISTRY COMMENCED WITH PRAYER

Dr. G. Campbell Morgan pointed out the fact that the word used in Luke 3:21-22 to express the activity of prayer is *proseuchomai,* which literally means to wish forward or to desire onward. It is the first mention of our Lord praying, and it is most revealing. He is seen in an attitude of devotion, desire, and dependence upon the Father and the Spirit. It was a prayer of faith and confidence. It looked forward to mighty achievements. That is the whole idea in that word *praying.*

In answer to Christ's prayer, the *Father approved* Him, the *Spirit anointed* Him, and the *people acknowledged* Him.

HIS MINISTRY CONTINUED WITH PRAYER

Mark tells about another occasion on which Christ prayed (Mark 1:35-38). The preceding day had been a very busy one for our Lord. He had taught in the synagogue (Mark 1:21-22), cast out demons (Mark 1:23-27), healed Peter's mother-in-law (Mark 1:30-31), and ministered to many who were sick (Mark 1:32-34). He had been pressured by crowds until late, making it an active, long and exhausting day. We can assume that the following morning He must have needed an extra hour's sleep. But instead, He arose while it was yet dark, slipped away to a quiet place, "and there prayed" (Mark 1:35).

We Christians cannot afford to neglect a quiet time alone with God at the beginning of each day. The servant is not greater than his Lord. If our lives and our efforts are to bring forth fruit that will remain, we need divine direction every day. If we make our plans ahead, let them be made only after we have prayed for God's leading. And even then, we must come daily to Him, because He might change our plans. Our sphere of activity for each new day must be preceded by prayer, so as to allow the Holy Spirit to choose for us. Just as our Savior would not choose His own program without first praying to the Father, neither should we. It is not possible for a Christian to know God's best for him apart from prayer.

HIS MINISTRY COUNTED UPON PRAYER

Some Christians experience a large measure of success, even to the extent of having fame and honor heaped upon them. The old, carnal nature, which is ever a part of us, thrives on the plaudits of our fellowmen. It becomes difficult for any of us to remain humble and dependent upon the Lord when we are being praised by others.

Jesus had enemies, but He also had many friends and followers—so many that He became famous. Now, note in Luke

5:15-16, what action He took. He withdrew into the wilderness and prayed. What a lesson there is here for us! I wonder if some of us might not be tempted to count on those many friends who honor and praise us. I imagine it could be quite hard for some of us not to succumb to this temptation. In that crisis, Christ counted on prayer.

When a Christian reaches a new peak of prosperity and prominence, it is time to withdraw himself and pray. Let me warn you that at just such a time we will not feel a great need to pray. We will be tempted to respond to those who speak well of us. But beware! A Christian being used of God can lose his power and usefulness if his heart is lifted up with pride. Prayer meant much to Jesus when fame came to Him; let us also count heavily on prayer in such a crisis.

Beloved Christian, let us never lose our sense of dependence upon God. We must count much on prayer, as did our Lord Jesus Christ. He retreated from the presence and plaudits of men in order to commune with the Father.

HIS MEN WERE CHOSEN IN PRAYER

It was in the plan and purpose of God that Jesus should choose twelve men who would represent Him after His departure. (Luke 6:12-13)

The selection of the twelve apostles was an important item of business, calling for prolonged communion with the Father. But why an all-night prayer meeting? Could not the selection of men have been made in less time? I know only that some requests are not granted at once. I know also that we tend to choose men on the basis of their outward appearances and personal preferences. Churches have been made to suffer great loss because the leaders did not spend enough time in prayer before calling a pastor. Paul warned Timothy, "Lay hands suddenly on no man" (I Timothy 5:22), and told him not to be guilty of prejudice and partiality (v. 21). It is important that God's man be chosen for God's work, and all such choices call for much prayer.

So burdened was our Lord for that solemn task, that He lost all sense of time and prayed on and on until the break of day. And with the new dawn there came the selection of the twelve, some of who became the penmen of much of the New Testament.

Such waiting upon God was practiced also by some in the early church. Luke writes of the apostles facing the selection of men to carry the gospel to new fields, "As they ministered to the Lord, and fasted, the Holy Ghost said, "Separate me Barnabas and Saul for the work whereunto I have called them.
And when they had fasted and prayed, and laid their hands on the, they sent them away" (Acts 13:2-3). And that is the way it should be done. Before any church selects a pastor, or elders, this example in the life of our Lord and of the early church should be given serious consideration.

HIS MIRACLES WERE CONSUMMATED BY PRAYER

The miracles of our Lord have had a strong appeal to the masses of people, both during His lifetime and up to our present day. But not much has been said or written about the relationship of those miracles to His prayer life. In our brief study we will examine two of Christ's miracles—the feeding of the five thousand men plus women and children, and the raising of Lazarus from death and the grave. These two incidents have been selected because they both pertain to the giving and sustaining of life.

Let us look first at the miracle He performed by feeding the multitude. The record of this miracle appears in Matthew, chapter 14; Mark, chapter 6; and John, chapter 6. Matthew and Mark both relate that He prayed before and after the miraculous feeding. His prayer was one of faith and confidence. "They did all eat and were filled" (Matthew 14:20).

> And when he had sent the multitudes away, he went up into a mountain apart to pray; and when the evening was come, he was there alone (Matthew 14:23).

That experience in the prayer life of our Lord is deeply instructive. It stands as an example for the prayer life of every child of God. As we meet God's requirements for successful praying, we can ask for our daily bread with the same confidence and assurance that God will supply every need. But be sure you do not miss the grand climax in the story—"He went up into a mountain apart to pray." He had received His request, but the prayer fellowship with His Father continued. Modern Christians grab the handout and say, "So long, God. I'll be back when I need more bread." I prefer to keep in constant touch with the Source of supply, as Jesus did.

We come now to the miracle of giving life to the dead. Only John recorded the miracle of raising Lazarus from death and the grave. Lazarus had been in the tomb four days. A large crowd had gathered, and they were mourning the death of this brother of Mary and Martha. When Jesus arrived at the tomb. He requested that the stone be removed. And then, looking upward, He prayed, "Father, I thank thee that thou hast heard me" (John 11:41).

This suggests that before He came to the tomb, He had already prayed about the raising of Lazarus, and the miracle that followed was an answer to that prayer. He was assured of the restoration of Lazarus's life because He was confident that the Father would grant the request. He continued to pray, "And I knew that thou hearest Me always" (John 11:42).

There lay the dead body. But Christ believed that God not only *could* but *would* restore life to Lazarus. His prayer was an intercessory one, and the request was granted. We know this because, "he that was dead came forth" (John 11:44). As our Lord performed this mightiest of miracles, He linked prayer and praise together. And on this occasion, all who were present were taught some precious lessons about prayer. That was the only reason Christ prayed and thanked the Father in the presence of the crowd standing there. He said,

> And I knew that thou hearest me always; but because of the people which stand by I said it, that they may believe that thou hast sent me (John 11:42).

HIS MINISTRY (ON EARTH) CONCLUDED IN PRAYER

He realized that the hour had come when He would be made the sin offering for us, and He would experience the awful loneliness of that separation from the Father. But He faced it triumphantly in prayer, in total submission to the divine will.

He went away again the second time, and prayed,
Saying, O my Father, if this cup may not pass away
From me, except I drink it, thy will be done (Mt 26:42).

We, too, can face life's bitter experiences in the will of God by surrendering our will in prayer. "The cup which my Father hath given me, shall I not drink it?" (John18: 11).

We move on to Calvary and those last moments before Christ's death on the cross. His first words in those dying moments were in the form of a prayer in behalf of those very men who had driven the nails through His hands and feet. He prayed, "Father, forgive them; for they know not what they do" (Luke 23:34).

Here is the classic example of an uncommon form of intercessory prayer. It is much easier to pray for ourselves, our loved ones, and our close friends than it is to pray for our enemies. But here we see our Lord at His best, praying for His enemies, who were putting Him to death. He was practicing what He had taught His followers in the Sermon on the Mount:

Love your enemies, bless them that curse you, do good to
them that hate you, and pray for them which despitefully
use you, and persecute you (Matthew 5:44).

And then His work on earth was complete. Having suffered for the sins of man, He breathed His last breath in a quiet prayer in behalf of those for who He was dying. And as He yielded up His life, He said, "Father, into thy hands I commend my spirit: (Luke 23:46).

This was His final prayer on earth. It was a prayer of confidence. I can think of no better way for a person to die than in sweet communion with God.

HIS MINISTRY (IN HEAVEN) CONTINUES IN PRAYER

When our Lord left earth and ascended to the Father, He did not cease to pray. He still prays.

Wherefore he is able also to save them to the uttermost that come unto God by him, seeing he ever liveth to make intercession for them (Hebrews 7:25).

Christ is a "priest for ever" (Hebrews 7:17), and He "continueth ever," having "an unchangeable priesthood" (Hebrews 7; 24). Therefore there is never a single moment when His prayers in our behalf do not reach our heavenly Father. He exercises the priestly function of His office without interruption or interference, so that all who are His can never be lost. He is able to save completely. He saved us by His propitiatory work in His death; He keeps us saved through His priestly work in heaven. The fruit of His propitiatory work is our salvation; the fruit of His priestly work is our security. In the performance of His priestly ministry, He does not live for Himself, but for all who have come to God through Him. He prays for our sake. That is what He is doing in heaven now.

Christ is our "great high priest" (Hebrews 4:14), yes, the greatest of high priests, whose prayers abound with the power of deity. No one ever prayed for us who is as glorious as our High Priest. His prayers are superior to the prayers of all the saints. Because He lives continuously, He intercedes continuously. The Christian gospel embraces the living Priest as well as the dying Savior. Christ reconciled us to God by His death (Romans 5:10), and He represents us before God in His life, "now to appear in the presence of God for us" (Hebrews 9:24). As Christ entreated the Father in behalf of Peter (Luke 22:31-32), so He intercedes at this very moment in our behalf. His present ministry of intercession and intervention is just as real and vital now as was His death on the cross for our sins. We are ever dependent upon our eternal Priest and His continuing prayers for us. **AMEN!**

Enclosure Seven – Praying: Selected Scriptures

Deuteronomy 4:4, 29-31	But you who held fast to the Lord your God are alive today, every one of you. But from there you will seek the Lord your God, and you will find Him if you search for Him with all your heart and all your soul. When you are in distress and all these things have come upon you, in the latter days you will return to the Lord your God and listen to His voice. For the Lord your God is a compassionate God; He will not fail you nor destroy you nor forget the covenant with your fathers, which He swore to them.
I Samuel 12:23	Moreover, as for me, far be it from me that I should sin against the Lord by ceasing to pray for you; but I will instruct you in the good and right way.
Psalm 50:14, 15	Offer to God a sacrifice of thanksgiving and pay your vows to the Most High: call upon Me in the day of trouble: I shall rescue you, and you will honor Me.
Psalm 55:16, 17	As for me, I shall call upon God; and the Lord will save me. Evening and morning and at noon, I will complain

	and murmur, and He will hear my voice.
Psalm 66:18	If I regard wickedness in my heart, the Lord will not hear;
Psalm 141:5	Let the righteous smite me in kindness and reprove me; it is oil upon the head; do not let my head refuse it, for still my prayer is against their wicked deeds.
Proverbs 15:8, 29	The sacrifice of the wicked is an abomination to the Lord: but the prayer of the upright is His delight. The Lord is far from the wicked, but hears the prayer of the righteous.
Isaiah 55:6	Seek the Lord while He may be found; call upon Him while He is near.
Jeremiah 29:11-13	For I know the plans I have for you, declares the Lord, plans for welfare and not for calamity to give you a future and a hope. Then you will call upon Me and come and pray to Me, and I will listen to you. You will seek Me and find Me when you search for Me with all your heart.
Jeremiah 33:3	Call to Me and I will answer you, and I will tell you great and mighty things, which you do not know.
Ezekiel 22:30	I searched for a man among them who would build up the wall and stand in the gap before Me for the

land, so I would not destroy it; but I found no one.

Matthew 5:44

But I say to you, love your enemies and pray for those who persecute you,

Matthew 6:6-15

But you, when you pray, go into your inner room, close your door and pray to your Father who is in secret, and your Father who sees what is done in secret will reward you. And when you are praying, do not use meaningless repetition as the Gentiles do, for they suppose they will be heard for their many words. So do not be like them; for your Father knows what you need before you ask Him.

"Pray, then, in this way:

Our Father who is in heaven,
Hallowed be Your name.
Your kingdom come,
Your will be done,
On earth as it is in heaven.
Give us this day, our daily bread.
And forgive us our debts, as we also have forgiven our debtors.
And do not lead us into temptation, but deliver us from evil.
For Yours is the kingdom and the power and glory forever.
Amen.

For if you forgive others for their transgressions, your heavenly Father will also forgive you. But if you do not forgive others, then your Father will not forgive your transgressions.

Matthew 7:7,8	Ask, and it will be given to you; seek and you will find; knock, and it will be opened. For everyone who asks receives, and he who seeks finds, and to him who knocks it will be opened.
Matthew 18:19, 20	Again I say to you, that if two of you agree on earth about anything that they may ask, it shall be done for them by my Father who is in heaven. For where two or three have gathered together in My name, I am there in their midst.
Mark 11:24, 25	Therefore I say to you, all things for which you pray and ask, believe that you have received them, and they will be granted you. Whenever you stand praying, forgive, if you have anything against anyone, so that your Father who is in heaven will also forgive you your transgressions.
Ephesians 6:18	With all prayer and petition pray at all times in the Spirit, and with this in view, be on the alert with all perseverance and petition for all the Saints,
Colossians 4:2	Devote yourselves to prayer, keeping alert in it with an attitude of thanksgiving;
I Thessalonians 5:17, 18	Pray without ceasing. In everything give thanks: for this is God's will for you in Christ Jesus.
I Thessalonians 5:23	Now may the God of peace Himself sanctify you entirely; and may your

	spirit and soul and body be preserved complete, without blame at the coming of our Lord Jesus Christ.
I Timothy 2:1,2	First of all, then, I urge that entreaties and prayers, petitions and thanksgivings, be made on behalf of all men, for kings and for all that are in authority, so that we may lead a tranquil and quiet life in all godliness and dignity.
II Timothy 2:7	Consider what I say, for the Lord will give you understanding in everything.
Philemon 4, 6	I thank my God always, making mention of you in my prayers, And I pray that the fellowship of your faith may become effective through the knowledge of every good thing, which is in you for Christ's sake.
Hebrews 4:16	Therefore let us draw near with confidence to the throne of grace, so that we may receive mercy and find grace to help in time of need.
James 4:7	Submit therefore to God. Resist the devil and he will flee from you.
James 5:14-18	Is anyone among you sick? Then he must call for the elders of the church and they are to pray over him, anointing him with oil in the name of the Lord; and the prayer offered in faith will restore the one who is sick,

and the Lord will raise him up, and if he has committed sins, they will be forgiven him. Therefore, confess your sins to one another, and pray for another, so that you may be healed. The effective prayer of a righteous man can accomplish much. Elijah was a man with a nature like ours, and he prayed earnestly that it would not rain, and it did not rain on the earth for three years and six months. Then he prayed again, and the sky poured rain and the earth produced its fruit.

1 John 1:9	But if we confess our sins to Him, He is faithful and just to forgive us our sins and to cleanse us from all wickedness.
Revelation 8:3,4	Another angel came and stood at the altar, holding a golden censer; and much incense was given to him, so that he might add it to the prayers of all the saints on the golden altar which was before the throne. And the smoke of the incense, with the prayers of the saints, went up before God out of the angel's hand.

Enclosure Eight –
Praying Evidences in the Bible

PRAYING EVIDENCE IN THE BIBLE

WORDS	O.T.	N.T.	TOTAL	UNIQUE	MEANINGS
CALL	50	6	56	Invite	Appeal
CALLED	51	2	53	"	"
CALLING	0	1	1	"	"
CALLS	2	1	3	"	"
COMPLAIN	1		1		
CRY	66	4	70	Cry out	Shout
CRYING	3	6	9	"	"
GROANING(S)	14	2	16		
MURMUR	1		1		
PRAY	57	49	106	Implore	Entreat
PRAYED	29	17	46	Supplicate	"
PRAYER	71	31	102	A whispering	Interview

PRAYERS	2	23	25	"	"
PRAYING	9	26	35	"	"
PRAYS	4	1	5	"	"
SEEK	72	13	85	Search	Seek
SEEKING	2	2	4	"	"
SEEKS	1	0	1	"	"
SOUGHT	20	2	22	"	"
TOTAL	**455**	**186**	**641**		